BOOMERS
—— AND ——
BEFORE
Real Stories from Yesterday's Children

Compiled by Nancy Burnette Fowler

Copyright © 2013 Individual contributors each own
their own copyrights

All rights reserved.
ISBN-13: 987-1492187486:
ISBN-10: 1492187488

DEDICATION

These real stories, told by yesterday's children, are dedicated to the children of today and tomorrow, in the hopes that they will grow and flourish without the disease of childhood cancer.

All proceeds from this book will be contributed to the Scott Carter Foundation, a foundation with the mission of raising funds for childhood cancer research. For more information, go to: www.scottcarterfoundation.org

CONTENTS

Acknowledgements	i
Explorers, Billy Burnette	1
Victims of the Law, Jon Kesler	10
An Indiana Courtship, The Wortmans	13
Milk Money, Tina Hackworth	19
The Milk Wars, Nancy Fowler	25
Resilience, Bob Grossman	29
George and Bob, Paul Compton	36
Driving at 12, Paul Compton	40
A Matter of Principle, Ann Zimmerman Crane	43
Independence, Margy Kesler	51
Water Conservation, Margaret Speke Davison	56
Leader of the Band, Margaret Speke Davison	59
The Mango Kid, Hank Fowler	63
Hot Beans, Hank Fowler	66
Robert the Robot, Kris Wells	69
Monkey in a Teacup, Kris Wells	73
A Hole in the Bucket, Nancy Fowler	76
Paper Boy, Keith Gant	84
Hair Revolt, Nadine Wells	89
Food and Fun, Talmadge Burnette, Sr.	94
Tootsie in Charge, Sandy Montgomery	98
The Fighting Field, Richard Burnette	101

"To walk through your memories takes courage, heart, love and the gift of understanding."

—*Keith Gant, "Don't Tell Mama"*

ACKNOWLEDGMENTS

Thank you to all of the folks who took the time to donate a story from their childhood or teen years for this book. It was my joy to read or listen to each story. I hope it was their joy to relish and share their memories.

Thank you also to all of the readers who bought this book. Your purchase will help support a very worthy cause—research for childhood cancer. I hope this collection of true stories brings back good memories from your own young years.

—Nancy Burnette Fowler

EXPLORERS
Billy Burnette
Swannanoa, North Carolina
1959

It's hard to tell the story of what we saw in the old Solesbee house without telling you something about Riddle Road first. It was just a mile or so of dirt road that turned off of Bee Tree Road near Swannanoa and ran up into a holler between Watch Knob and the Three Brothers along a little no-name creek that eventually ran into the Swannanoa River.

I say "dirt road" even though it was technically a county gravel road, because the gravel wasn't replenished often. It was muddy in the winter and dusty in the summer, and the grownups often talked about how the county should gravel it more often, and how it would be nicer still if they actually paved it someday.

But when I grew up there, it was mostly dirt, and that didn't bother us kids at all. In my memory, Riddle Road didn't belong to the grownups anyhow. It was ours. We were its original inhabitants, its discoverers, the mappers of its unknown reaches and the conquistadors who went in search of its treasures. That little creek might just as well have been a river tributary snaking deep into some Amazonian jungle—and it was peopled at intervals with wild adolescent tribes.

The big Allen tribe was just up the road from my home, near the end of navigation (or Where the School Bus Turned Around, as we called it)—Denver, Shelby, Emory, Shirley, Merle, and Gerald, in descending order. We called Merle and Gerald "Murl 'n' Jurl." The Allens were an agricultural tribe. They farmed tobacco, plowing the fields behind a mule and hauling the tobacco to a tall barn on a wooden sled. They were hard-working kids, not as free to roam as the rest of us in the summer because of farm chores.

There was a tribe of McGees down near the last big curve before Riddle Road dead-ended in a lethal blind intersection with Bee Tree Road—Jane, Jim, and Bill. They lived on the other side of the creek from the road, and had a bike-chasing dog who would come across the plank bridge like a cheetah whenever we passed, looking until the last instant as if he were going to take us down like kudu on the South African veldt, and then falling in behind to chase us until he was sure he driven us from McGee territory.

Kathleen, LoRitha, and Kenny Jenkins were another farming tribe, separated from the road by their fields and tucked away in the shadow of the Three Brothers, three adjoined mountains that helped create the holler. There were Taylors and McDowells as well, and Lunsfords and Drakes, each tribe with its own territory, customs, peculiarities, and lore. Among these tribes were rivalries and alliances, and sometimes out-right war.

I was of the Burnette tribe. Our lands were high up a rutted driveway that skirted the Allen tribe's tobacco field and pasture on the Watch Knob side. There were three of us—my older brother Malcolm, me, and my younger sister Cindy. Montagnards, I guess you could call us, hunter-gathers who did a little subsistence gardening. We were one of two Burnette tribes.

Down past the Jenkins at the widest point of the little valley that the holler spilled out into were cousins of ours:

Butch, Richard, Nancy, and Bruce. They were a herding and fishing tribe, with horses and a milk cow and a barn and pasture, a stock pond with bream and sunfish in it.

They could be fierce rivals in the bike and sled races and the snowball and pine-cone fights, and they were canny operators who often got the best of us in the main form of intertribal commerce—trading comic books. But the other tribes knew that if you messed with one of the Burnette tribes, you were messing with both of them. We had each other's backs. However, as you're about to hear, it was sometimes unwise to turn our backs on each other.

Surrounded as you are today by multiplexes and malls and smart phones and hundreds of cable channels, you might be surprised at how much there was to do on a narrow rural track on its way to nowhere.

In the winter we built snow forts on hillsides, engineered to give us good fields of fire, and caromed down the same steep slopes on unguidable sleds we made ourselves. In the spring we fished in the stock pond. In the summer we cut wild grapevines loose from their roots and swung out over deep ravines on them until they dried out and broke loose from the branches of their hosts and dropped us into the brush below.

We climbed the middle of the Three Brothers to an abandoned mica mine that zigzagged back into darkness. We made cheese sandwiches and Kool-Aid and spread old quilts in the shade at the edge of our yards and read adventure novels and comic books. We walked for hours, head down in the summer heat, through the plowed fields at the lower end of the road, picking up flint and obsidian arrowheads and shards of pottery left by tribes that had lived along the creek long before us.

And in the fall, we boys would tumble down out of the school bus and lope to our rooms for our shotguns or .22 rifles and climb through the leaf-bright woods to the hickory stands on the ridges and hunt squirrels.

It was one midsummer day—when the arrowhead fields were covered over with crops, and all the comic books we had in stock had been traded and read by every tribe on the road, and we'd run out of grapevines and tired of fishing and riding our bikes—that cousin Butch called and said he had some excitement planned. Although Butch was oddly insistent, we had lawn-mowing to do, and our mother wouldn't let us go.

The following day, Butch called again, and Malcolm asked just what it was that was so all-fired important that he'd keep pestering us about it. "Exploring," Butch said. "Me and Richard are going exploring, and we want you to come along."

"Exploring what?" Malcolm asked.

"Just exploring," Butch said. "We found a new place. Just come on down. You'll see." Even our mother had begun to wonder what it was all about, so we were soon on our way.

When we got there, Butch was releasing information on a strictly need-to-know basis, and answered all our questions with, "You'll see." Richard claimed to be as uninformed as Malcolm and I were. We set off across the road and the pasture toward the stock pond, with no fishing poles or firearms or other gear that would give us any clue as to what was up.

Beyond the stock pond, a tall, well-maintained barbed-wire fence marked the boundary of Burnette territory, and while we were no respecters of fences and property lines, we had never ranged far in this direction. We knew that there was an old road back in the woods, and that a brother and sister named Solesbee had once lived somewhere along it. But whatever sort of dwelling they'd lived in was far enough into the woods to be concealed even when the leaves were off the trees.

We followed Butch ever deeper into the woods, until he stopped and held up a hand like an infantry point man. Through the summer foliage, we could just see the outline of a little house, black tarpaper on the roof, walls unpainted and weathered. "This is it," Butch whispered.

It was pretty clear as we got closer that the place was abandoned. The windows were boarded up, and the road that ran past behind it was deep in seasons and seasons of leaf fall. But we crept up on it as if there were people in it and we intended to take them unaware. "The old Solesbee place," Butch whispered. "The door's on the other side."

Even with bright sunlight spilling through the poplar and oak leaves and birds singing in the woods around us, the old house had a foreboding mien. The boarded windows seemed intended to conceal secrets rather than merely keep out the rain. The uninterrupted carpet of decaying leaves that surrounded it said that people didn't go there anymore, and maybe weren't welcome. And even before we got close, there was an unpleasant smell surrounding it.

There was no reason whatsoever to be quiet, but we had fallen into Butch's mood of hushed apprehension, and we followed him around the house in single file, looking nervously into the woods around us as if something were out there, watching and waiting.

The door faced the abandoned road. There was a single step up, and we filed in, and found ourselves in near darkness. As our eyes adjusted to the gloom, we saw a rough counter with an old porcelain sink in the center of it.

The floor was dingy, cracked linoleum, grey with age and dirt. The walls were bare except for yellowing newspapers and magazine pages held in place by flaking adhesive. A tin plate with a winter scene painted on it covered a hole high in the wall where a stovepipe had been.

We were in what had been the kitchen, and it was hardly big enough for all of us, and the smell, whatever it was, was stronger. A door led into another room. Malcolm went to the sink and turned on the faucet with no results, and Butch said, "Come on. There's nothing in here. Let's see what's in the other rooms."

The next room was even darker than the first. The floor was bare boards, and there were scraps of newspaper that had peeled off the walls and small artifacts to indicate that people had in fact once lived there, an old cap, a cold-cream jar, a rusted bottle opener with a cracked wooden handle. Dark grey dust covered portions of the floor, and it was gritty underfoot. The room was hardly larger than the kitchen, but it must have been the main room of the house. There was another door, too. This one was closed, and there was a hasp on it, with a coat hanger twisted through to keep it shut.

Butch went directly to the door. "What do you reckon's in here?" he said.

"I don't know," Malcolm said, "but it looks like somebody doesn't want anybody to go in. Maybe we should leave it alone."

"Nah," Butch said. "Nobody's lived here for years. Anyhow, we came to explore, didn't we? Go ahead and open it."

Malcolm stepped up to the door and started reluctantly to untwist the coat hanger. I was standing on tiptoe trying to read one of the faded newspapers when I heard the hanger clatter to the floor and felt the draft of the door swinging inward, and when I looked, Malcolm and Butch were gone, and Richard was standing looking in the door. I heard footsteps in the unlocked room, and heard Butch whisper "Look over there. What is that?"

There was a scuffling sound, and Butch shouted, and Malcolm burst from the room, nearly knocking Richard over, and ran through the door into the kitchen, the house shaking from the pounding of his feet. I heard the kitchen door slam against the outside wall, and then heard Malcolm's running footsteps in the leaves as he rounded the house.

Butch and Richard were right behind him, and I was left standing in the middle of the room, still looking at the coat hanger lying on the floor beside the open door. Whatever Butch had shouted, the words hadn't registered. Torn between following the others and finding out why they'd fled,

I went to the door and stepped just inside it, waiting for my eyes to adjust to the darker gloom, and gradually a cot emerged from the shadows in the corner, a threadbare blanket thrown across it.

Something was lying under the blanket on the cot. Boots stuck out on the end nearer the door. There was the shape of legs and a torso and arms, distorted and grotesque. And at the other end of the cot, the vague outline of a face, covered by the blanket also, a nose making a tiny tent in the fabric in the middle of it. Suddenly I knew what Butch had shouted. He had said, "It's a dead man!" And it was time for me to run.

As the smallest and last to leave, I was far behind the others. When I got to their house, I found Butch and Richard strangling with laughter and Malcolm scowling in anger. And it took a while for me to gather from the conversation what had just happened.

We should have known, of course. It followed a familiar pattern. Butch was always a prankster, and Malcolm his favorite victim.

The old Solesbee house, it seems, was not at all new to Butch and Richard. They had been playing there, unbeknownst to their parents, all summer, shooting at the cans and bottles discarded around the house with BB guns. They had discovered that the smell came from the mysterious powder on the floor, and more mysterious still, if you poured water on it, it smoked. (It turned out to be calcium carbide that the Solesbees had used in lamps, and the "smoke" was acetylene gas generated by a chemical reaction with the water. Had they ever struck a match to see the fumes better in the gloom, this might have been a more tragic story.)

They had also used materials they'd found in the house to construct the "dead man." The legs were stovepipes, the torso an old washtub turned upside down, the head a pile of rags with a washer to make the nose.

Malcolm later told me that Butch had shoved him toward the cot when he shouted, and that there was something slippery on the floor of the room—cold cream, maybe—and scared as he was already, he was a lot more scared by the time he got enough traction to get out of the room. According to Butch and Richard, Malcolm had jumped the fence without breaking stride, streaked past the pond and through the pasture and across the road, and burst into our cousins' house shouting to Aunt Blanche that he had to call the sheriff. Our cousins had put on a burst of speed themselves, because they had to get there in time to stop him.

The dead man in the old Solesbee house became one of the tribal legends of Riddle Road, raising Butch to the status of Supreme Shaman of Practical Jokes and spreading beyond the tribal territories when school started in the fall. But the last laugh was on Butch after all.

Before he got around to disassembling his tin zombie, Roy Solesbee, who had moved to an even smaller and more run-down house further up the old road, happened by his previous home and went inside. When he saw the dummy, he ran to the house of one Mr. Greene, who lived not far from the cousins, and together they returned to the house. Mr. Greene carried a cane, and his response to the dead man was to give him a sturdy whack with it.

When the blow was greeted with a clank rather than a thud, the secret was out. He went home and called the sheriff, who came to investigate, and it was our Aunt Blanche who got our revenge for us by telling Butch and Richard that the sheriff had been around asking about the dummy, and they were probably in big trouble.

That was more than 50 years ago. Riddle Road is paved now, and you can look at it on Google Maps. It doesn't seem to go any further into the mountains than it did then, but there are more houses and they're bigger. Like me, a lot of the kids who lived there have left Western North Carolina altogether. But I hope that there are still tribes, and that they still have adventures. And I hope someone on Riddle Road remembers the story of the dead man in the old Solesbee house.

Postscript:
The Burnette cousins continued their adventures until each left Riddle Road to embark upon adulthood. Bill gave seven years to the U.S. Army, serving in Vietnam. He then graduated from San Jose State University with a BA and MA in English literature. He has worked as an English teacher, marketing writer and novelist. His first novel, "The Long Roll", intertwines the Civil War, Vietnam and the current war on terrorism. His second book, "Christmas in Sunny California," is a touching (and often funny) holiday story that can be found on amazon.com by searching on W.E. Burnette or Christmas in Sunny California.

VICTIMS OF THE LAW
Jon Kesler
Iron River, Wisconsin
1961 to 1967

The dairy lobby had an enormous impact on my family during the late 1950s and early 1960's. As the "Dairy State", Wisconsin passed laws to protect the state's dairy farmers from competition with non-dairy substitutes. My family had roots in the dairy industry—my mother was the daughter of a cheese maker and dairy farmer—but that didn't stop the oleo-butter contest from causing a serious inconvenience to the Kesler parents and providing a great adventure for the three Kesler sons.

Our adventure started when I was three, and my father, at age 50, had a major heart attack. My family feared the worst and his doctor indicated that he might not recover. It was a frightening time for the Keslers. My father spent weeks in the hospital and then more weeks recovering in his bed at home as part of his doctor's prescribed treatment.

My father's doctor was adamant that he had to cut out all fats, including his cherished butter. Oleo, also known as oleomargarine, was the recommended substitute (this was before we knew about transfats). However, we lived in Wisconsin, the dairy state. The dairy industry insisted that adding yellow coloring to oleo was confusing and dishonest to consumers and that any competition to real dairy products should be heavily taxed in order to maximize income to the state's dairy farmers. Nationally, these laws were being repealed, but not in the dairy state. As a result, Wisconsin oleo was extremely expensive and remained its original unappetizing pasty white color. It looked a bit like lard, not something you would enjoy spreading on your toast each morning. The laws made it clear that no untaxed, yellow oleo was to be brought into our state. Rather than eat the pale, extremely expensive version that was available to us, we opted to break the law. Every few months we drove 65 miles to Ironwood, Michigan to buy large cartons of beautiful yellow, and cheap, oleo.

We weren't the only family with a member whose fat intake was restricted and who decided to purchase the non-butter spread from out-of-state and illegally bring it back to our state. In fact, an entire oleo-smuggling syndicate had developed in our small town. We took turns "running" oleo, and if anyone was going to Michigan (Minnesota was out of the question as it had its own laws) they did the neighborly thing, asking if anyone needed a few cases of oleo. We all had large freezers and a good portion of each freezer was dedicated to the family oleo stash.

When it was our turn to make the drive, my brothers and I piled into our 1957 blue and white Plymouth Fury station wagon. We looked forward to the trips, not only for the sight-seeing they afforded, but also because my father built up the drama, risk and adventure of the trip, telling us that if we were stopped for speeding on our way back, we were to remain very quiet, not indicating that there was anything in the back of our station wagon. My brothers and I saw the trips as risky business; our family was breaking the law and we were participants. After buying several cases of oleo at a Michigan grocery store, we stacked the boxes in the back of the Plymouth and my dad carefully covered them with a blanket. Then we started the trip home with the contraband just a few inches behind my and my brothers' heads and shoulders. Every time we passed a sheriff's or highway patrol car, my brothers and I sucked in our breath and looked at each other, our hearts beating a little faster, careful not to even glance at the back of the station wagon, for fear that an officer of the law would detect an on-going crime from five cars away.

When we returned to Iron River, we made our oleo drops to our friends and neighbors and collected our take. Once we had the oleo in the house, all of the adventure surrounding it evaporated and it became just another food product. However, it remained the only spread for our rolls and the only type of fat that my mother used for cooking.

An interesting thing about the oleo-smuggling syndicate members, all of them, including my parents, were not rule-breakers by nature. They were law-abiding, church-going citizens who didn't so much as drink or smoke. I never quite determined whether they were drawing the line on how much the government could control their lives, or if they just wanted to buy oleo, a healthier alternative to butter, at reasonable prices. Whatever the reason, their breaking the law gave their three sons an unforgettable adventure.

Postscript:
Wisconsin dropped the oleo tax and color-added laws in 1967. There is no record of any arrests for bringing out-of-state oleo into Wisconsin. When asked what spread is in his refrigerator today, Jon responded, "Butter—whoever heard of hot-margarined rum?" Happily, Jon did not grow up to be an outlaw butter-runner, but an Organizational Change Management professional, lending his professional skills and experience to federal agencies.

AN INDIANA COURTSHIP
Royal and Don Wortman
Evansville Indiana
1947

Royal:
When I was in eighth grade, our grade school's basketball team made the play-offs. We had a particularly close game with a school that was about 10 miles from my school. Of course, all of my classmates and I showed up to cheer for our team. With only a few minutes to go in the game, the score was tied. The last basket was made by one of the shorter members of the opposing team, but he really was the best player. I later learned that his name was Don Wortman, but all of his friends called him "Duck." Because of his basketball talents, he was also known as the "Terror on the Court."

Don:
We were competing for the city school district championship of the rural schools that year. Unfortunately, we didn't win that championship; our center had problems with free throws. Both Royal and I went to rural grade schools that fed into the same consolidated high school, Reitz

High School. My grade school was close by my home, but Reitz High was a long bus ride, so when I started high school, it took me a full hour to get to school.

Royal:

It wasn't such a long ride for me; I lived closer to town. Freshman year was a big deal. I dated a few boys that year. Duck was in two of my classes; I knew who he was, but he didn't know me at all. We didn't talk to each other, and coming from different grade schools, we had different friends.

Don:

One spring day, a friend stopped me in the hall as we were changing classes. He asked me if I knew Royal Criswell. I didn't know her, so I said no. He insisted that I must know who she was, that she was in my biology class and sat right across from our friend Joan. He went on to say that he thought Royal was very pretty and that he wanted to ask her for a date for the coming weekend, but he was too shy. He wanted me to ask her for him. I agreed and then when I sat down at my biology class desk, I figured out who she was. My friend was right—she was very pretty. After class, I spoke to her, "Royal!", she turned and said, "yeah?" I said, "What are you doing this Saturday?" She replied, "Nothing." So I asked her, "Do you want to go with me to a movie?" And she said, "OK." So I went back to my friend and said, "Sorry, Royal is busy this Saturday night." Fortunately, he didn't hold it against me and we stayed friends.

I went home and told my dad I needed the car Saturday night. He said that he and my mom needed it for a cards party, but I could have the company truck. My dad owned an electrical business. He had a big blue and orange truck that had cables in the back, lots of them just dangling off the side of the truck. The company logo was painted on the doors, "Wortman Electric", and there was a big streak of lightning that was painted on the door so that it looked like the lightning was hitting the name. I didn't like the idea of taking the truck on a date, especially my first date with Royal. It was embarrassing.

Royal:
When Duck came to the door to pick me up, I could tell that the truck embarrassed him. He apologized, but it really didn't bother me a bit. I was fine with it. I just got into the truck and we went to the movie. That truck bothered Duck so much that he wouldn't park in front of the theater; he parked on a side street. I can't remember much about the movie, but I do remember how nervous Duck was. I could tell he hadn't dated a lot. I didn't have a good time and I decided I wouldn't go out with him again. We were both pretty young; I was only 15 and Duck was 16 but I'd dated several boys. It wasn't a big deal to me.

Don:
I'd never been to a movie before. I never had time. We lived pretty far out on a farm north of Evansville, Indiana and had lots of work to do. We went to Lawrenceville, Illinois maybe once a year, but there wasn't much opportunity to go anywhere. My dad's electrical business kept him and my brother busy. When the high-powered electrical line came in, my dad wired everything north of Evansville, all the way and all around to Darmstadt, a little town settled by German immigrants, giving him about a 20-mile circumference of wiring jobs. While they did the electrical work, I was responsible for the farm. We had 90 head of beef cattle and I had to take care of them. The cattle had to be fed. Our cattle ate well—timothy grass and clover hay, good quality grain. I gave them corn every night and put malt in it—made their fur look nice and shiny. Once a year, we'd load the cattle up and take them to a meat packer. They liked our cattle. We produced prime beef and we were paid top dollar. With all that work going on, I didn't have time to go places or date much.

Royal:
After that first date, he asked me out again and I told him I was busy. He didn't give up; he asked me out about three more times. I finally told him that the next time I had a free evening I'd give him a call. He got the hint that I didn't have a great time and I didn't hear from him again.

Our freshman year ended and I was dating other boys. One of my dates that summer took me to the Scott Township Vanderburg county fair. I love ice cream and he asked me if I wanted an ice cream cone, so I said sure! We walked over to the ice cream stand and there behind the counter was Duck, scooping ice cream.

Don:
And I gave her a four-dipper high ice cream cone. I'd pretty much put any thoughts of dating her again out of my mind, but seeing her at the county fair revved up my interest. I decided I'd give her one more chance. I was headed out squirrel hunting in a couple of Saturdays and asked her if she wanted to come along. I'm not sure what was going through my mind, but I figured I was going hunting anyway, so maybe she'd like to come.

Royal:
He asked me to go squirrel hunting! I'd never been and that interested me. It wasn't a usual date, but that's what I liked about it.

Don:
I told her to be ready at five in the morning, because you have to be sitting down by a tree before the sun comes up.

Royal:
He explained that when you go squirrel hunting, you have sit quietly by a tree before the squirrels start moving around;

you don't want them to know you are there. If you get there after sunup, they see you. It all sounded quite interesting.

But, that Saturday I overslept. Around six am, Daddy hollered upstairs and woke me up, "Royal, are you supposed to be someplace today?" I was still asleep, so I just mumbled, "No, why?" Daddy said, "Because there's a boy asleep in the porch swing!" That really woke me up. I started racing around, getting dressed and running outside. I had ruined our chances of getting into the woods before sunup.

We went anyway, even though it was too late to hunt squirrels. We walked deep into the woods and it was beautiful. Duck had fixed a picnic of cheese and crackers, sandwiches, cookies and marshmallows. It was quite nice! We had a great time and I really enjoyed his company. We laughed and talked a lot. He was so funny. In the woods, he was in his element and could be himself. The movies didn't do it, but the deep woods did. I knew I wanted to date him again.

Don:

After a few days, I asked her out again, but she said no! She said she had hives, but I thought, here we go again. She seemed to have had a good time on our squirrel hunting date, but I just wasn't sure if she was telling the truth about having hives or not. I drove by her house just to make sure no other boy's car was there.

Royal:

I really did have hives. We had canned peaches and I was eating all the broken slices—lots of broken slices. I didn't realize that too many peaches could cause hives and I broke all over. It was awful. I looked awful and I felt awful. I couldn't go to the movies; I couldn't go anywhere. I've never had hives since then, but I sure had them then. Fortunately, I recovered, and after that, we went to ballgames, movies, most everywhere together. I still dated other boys my sophomore and junior years, but I knew he was the one. Starting senior year, we went steady and have been going steady ever since.

Postscript:
Royal and Don were married in 1952. They farmed in Dale, Indiana until Don joined the Air Force. After his service, he became an air traffic controller and retired after 28 years. Royal worked as assistant manager of the Waffle House of Indiana Inc. headquarters. For about five years, Duck was equipment manager of Waffle House of Indiana. He then went back to working part-time as an air controller. Together they raised three beautiful children. In April of 2013, Royal and Don celebrated their sixty-third wedding anniversary.

MILK MONEY
Tina Hackworth
Lansing, Michigan
1959

Some children are just shy by nature. Others are shy because of where they fall in birth order, with middle children usually leaning towards reserved personalities. I got the double whammy—the middle of seven children and born with an already shy nature. I never felt shy with friends and family, although I was usually on the quiet side even in familiar surroundings. I was an observer, not a participator. In most situations, I didn't make waves, but just watched. I was sort of an "invisible" child and I really wanted to stay that way, but during first grade, grown-up forces began to merge and break the protective wrapping that kept me invisible, whether I liked it or not.

In the late 50's and early 60's, schools drew a correlation between nourishment and successful schoolwork. Children who were well nourished had a better chance at school success. For that reason, all first graders at our local school were given a mid-morning milk break. Each student had to pay for the milk a month at a time. To ensure that no child would go without their daily carton of good nutrition, the teachers sent home notes reminding parents when milk money was due. Unfortunately, the effort to create well-nourished and academically successful children almost had the opposite effect on me.

The first week of first grade, my mother put my milk money in an envelope and pinned it to the collar of my dress so that I wouldn't lose it. The amount wasn't much, a small collection of coins that slid to the lowest corner of the envelope. As I walked to school with my older brother Jack, who was supposed to keep an eye out for me between our house and the school, the coins lightly jingled in the envelope with each step I took. Jack's guardianship really wasn't needed. He was only one grade ahead of me and was more my peer than a protective or authoritative figure. Plus, all of the neighborhood kids walked together, so there was no danger. But still, Jack was responsible for me, so he obediently walked by my side every morning, although I was sure he preferred to be walking with other second graders.

Shortly after turning over my milk money to my teacher, Mrs. Fisher, it became evident to me that I could not participate in the daily milk break. The teacher had a list of milk money payers, which was just about the entire class, minus the children whose families could not afford the small monthly payment. A big crate of white and brown milk cartons was delivered to our class around 10 am each morning. With the crate sitting beside her desk, Mrs. Fisher read down the milk list, crisply calling out each name. After the child walked to the front of the classroom, he or she told the teacher "white" or "chocolate" and received a carton of milk. It happened fast, with lots of kids walking up and down the aisles at the same time. As I realized that I would have to walk to the front of the classroom and speak out loud, in front of the entire class, I knew that I couldn't do it. I loved chocolate milk more than anything, but I couldn't bear the thought of my classmates watching me walk to the front of the class, listening to me say my choice of milk out loud, although all that was required was one word. So, that first day of milk break, when the teacher called my name. I said, "no thank you" in a voice so quiet, she probably had to strain to hear me. Mrs. Fisher paused and looked over her glasses at me. "Tina, dear, you have paid for the milk. Wouldn't you like to come up and get your carton?" I looked at my desk and whispered, "I don't like milk." The very thought of walking to the front of the room and saying "chocolate" and then walking back to my desk sent waves of anxiety through me. I was sure every eye in the room would be on me, even as I drank my milk. Every day for the next month, we repeated this exchange, Mrs. Fisher asking me to come up and get my milk and me quietly responding that I didn't like milk.

After four weeks, all first graders took home the notes reminding our parents that milk money was due. I dutifully gave my mother the note and she dutifully pinned the milk money to my dress collar. As I walked to school with my brother Jack, my six-year-old brain worked out a solution that would remove all attention from me and free me from the dread of having my name called out by Mrs. Fisher. I unpinned the envelope from my collar and gave it to Jack. He looked at me in surprise and asked me why was I giving him the money. I told him I didn't like milk—he could go buy candy. He was pretty happy to be on the receiving end of such a windfall, quickly pocketed the envelope and didn't question the gift any further.

The plan didn't work as well as I thought it would. Mrs. Fisher collected everyone's milk money, except mine and that of one other child, "Jane", whose family could not afford the milk payment. I really hadn't paid attention, but Mrs. Fisher always made sure that Jane received a carton of milk—probably the carton I had just rejected. As time for milk break approached, I sat confidently thinking that I could relax and not have attention brought to me. Mrs. Fisher picked up the milk list, quickly reading out names. Children briskly walked to the front, confidently saying "white" or "chocolate" in strong clear voices, and going back to their desks to enjoy their cartons. I happily sat drawing with a new box of Crayola crayons, selecting my favorite colors and not paying attention to the movement around me. Then, my heard my name called. I couldn't quite believe it. I looked up from my paper and Mrs. Fisher was indeed looking at me. "Tina, dear, we have absent students today and I have extra milk. Would you like to take it?" The room had turned unusually quiet and I could feel the eyes of my classmates on me. My plan had miserably backfired. My face burned. I quickly shook my head no and whispered, "I don't like milk" and looked down at my hands. Mrs. Fisher didn't push the offer and the room returned to sounds of first graders enjoying their milk and six-year-old conversation. The next several days brought the same results. I had made my situation worse, calling even more attention to myself instead of deflecting it. My stomach was in knots by the time I arrived at school each morning, dreading milk break.

Mrs. Fisher liked to meet with each first-grader's parents and most parents showed up for the meeting. My parents were extremely busy working and caring for seven children, but my mother always showed up for teacher meetings. At this first meeting, Mrs. Fisher brought the milk subject up with my mother. But the information exchange between teacher and parent did not go smoothly. Neither woman understood what the other one was trying to say.

My mother was an extremely proud person. If any of her children depicted in any way that our family didn't have money, then that child had crossed a boundary that my mother would not tolerate. During the meeting, my mother was sure that Mrs. Fisher was inferring that our family could not afford milk money. It was very important for my mother that no one would ever point to her children and say, "Those kids are poor." She was the major breadwinner for our family, working three jobs to make sure her children were well taken care of. Our friends probably thought we had lots of money, but it was all smoke and mirrors created by my mother. We were by no means impoverished, but like most of the families who lived in our town, our money was tight. My mother feared that my rejection of milk would make our family appear to be in the same economic category as Jane's family. In reality, Mrs. Fisher probably didn't see my behavior in a financial light, but just wanted to bring me out of my shyness.

After that meeting, my mother made it clear to me that I had to get milk at school; there were no other options. My mother let me know that, in no uncertain terms, I would give my milk money to my teacher, and when she said my name, I had to walk to the front of the classroom, say white or chocolate, walk back to my desk and drink my milk.

As I walked to school the next day, with my milk money pinned to my collar and anxiety churning in my stomach almost to the point of throwing up, I couldn't imagine how I was going to get through milk break. Jack walked along beside me, not so sympathetic, but feeling his loss of candy money. Morning lessons went way too fast. As Mrs. Fisher pulled the milk list from her desk, my heart started thumping in my chest. She quickly went down the list, reaching my name. As terrified as I was to walk to the front of the room, I was even more terrified of my mother. It was the longest walk I had ever made in my six years. I walked with my head down, looking at my feet so that I didn't have to look at my classmates. I finally reached the front of the room, whispered "chocolate" and received my carton of milk. The trip back to my desk wasn't as bad; my ordeal was almost over. By the time I sat back down at my desk, I felt like the entire class was looking at me, so I only drank a couple of sips and threw away the rest of the milk. As the days and weeks went on, it became easier to walk to the front, return to my desk and drink all of my milk. By Christmas, it wasn't difficult at all and I looked forward to milk break.

By the time I reached fifth grade, my extreme shyness was a thing of the past. Our school had a talent contest and my mother encouraged me to try out. I liked to sing and had plenty of experience in children's choirs, but had never performed a solo. I willingly and hopefully added my name to the audition list as a soloist. My song was "He's Got the Whole World in His Hands" and my audition was in front of a group of teachers. My mother coached me, refining my hand gestures, making suggestions and encouraging me in a way that built my confidence. I was selected for our class's solo and not only sang in front of the entire fifth grade assembly, but also for the night performance attended by parents. It was easy and it was fun. And best of all, I loved the applause. Being invisible was a thing of the past. I discovered that stepping out in front was better.

Postscript:
Tina continued to grow as an outgoing individual. After retiring from the Ingham Intermediate School District school, Tina now helps out with the family timber business and enjoys her five grandchildren.

THE MILK WARS
Nancy Burnette Fowler
Swannanoa, North Carolina
1958

Like most kids in the fifties, my brothers and I were told to drink our milk. The adult reasoning given to us was that it would either make us grow tall, be strong or give us pretty teeth. For several years, we happily complied, enjoying fresh milk that came from our own cows, while we tried to be strong, grow tall, and have pretty teeth. We didn't quite accomplish all three goals (in fact, I failed miserably at all three) but the milk sure did taste good with Mom's chocolate sauce cake. However, in my ninth year of childhood, my three brothers and I hit a rough spot in our enjoyment of milk.

We were rural kids and for many years Dad milked every morning and every night. We went through a succession of Bessies and Bossies, cows that gave sweet creamy milk. Sometimes I followed Dad to the barn and even tried my hand at milking, although not so successfully. After the milk pail was full and the cow was empty, Dad covered the bucket with a clean towel and we walked back down the hill to the house. He handed the milk over to Mom who was waiting at the kitchen door. Only after the bucket was safely in her hands did he take off his barn boots and step inside. She took the bucket and poured the milk into glass bottles and sat them on the kitchen table. After a while, thick yellow cream collected at the top of the bottle. Mom spooned the cream off the top and put the rest of the milk into the refrigerator, making it easily accessible for our mealtime glass and morning cereal bowl.

The care and feeding of the cows took up a lot of Dad's daily routine—milking, feeding, cleaning the barn and sometimes chasing the cows out of the wild onion patch in order to prevent tainted milk with a flavor that my brothers and I could not abide. No cajoling about strong bones and pretty teeth could convince us to drink onion-flavored milk.

At some point during my third grade school year, our daily routine dramatically shifted. Dad took a full-time job with a small business that combined selling insurance policies and home fuel oil. He wasn't home as much as before and didn't have the time to milk. The milk cows were sold and were replaced by a metal box that sat on our front porch. A local dairy delivered chilled bottled milk to this box several times a week. Although this milk had a slightly different flavor, probably due to pasteurization, it never tasted like onions, and my brothers and I were happy enough to drink it.

After a couple of months of the dairy milk, Mom looked at the household budget and decided that delivered milk was a luxury we could not afford. She bought a few gallons from the grocery store—another taste shift for us—but soon decided that store-bought milk wasn't cost effective either. I knew that some of my friends' families were drinking powdered milk, a concoction of water and white granules that didn't look much different than powdered laundry detergent, but I never thought it would be sitting on our dinner table. I was wrong.

Mom made a big effort to sell us on the concept. She set the blue and white box of powdered milk on the kitchen table, along with a measuring cup and a milk bottle. My younger brother, Bruce, and I watched as she carefully measured and mixed, all the while using her cheeriest voice to tell us how we wouldn't know the difference and how much money this milk was going to save us. Once she combined the powder with the water, she poured a little in a glass for each of us. We carefully sipped the milk and I could tell that she was anxious and hopeful that the new milk could be declared a taste success. It wasn't to be; it didn't taste like milk at all, but instead like some strange, lukewarm liquid with an odd smell. Worse yet, on my first sip I took in a powdered lump that hadn't dissolved in the water. I wanted to spit it back into the glass, but knew if I did, I'd probably be sent to my room, so after mushing the lump between my tongue and the top of my mouth, I swallowed and then looked at Bruce. He was staring into his glass of "milk" and the distaste for it was all over his face. Mom knew the verdict without even asking, but she maintained her positive outlook by telling us, "It will taste so much better once it's chilled", and she put the bottle in the refrigerator. We knew it wouldn't taste better and it didn't. My older brothers were even more vocal than Bruce and I were, letting mom know that powdered milk was not "real" milk and it tasted terrible.

Mom kept trying for a few more days, pouring the mixture over our corn flakes, stirring it into our oatmeal, and placing glasses of the stuff next to our dinner plates. She even tried pairing it with her chocolate sauce cake. Ever the optimist, she was sure we would adapt to the new taste. It wasn't to be. The corn flakes went soggy, the oatmeal went cold, the mealtime glasses went untouched, and even chocolate sauce cake just wasn't the same. Then, one day we opened the refrigerator and there sat two store-bought gallons of milk. We had missed real milk and quickly consumed the first gallon. Almost as soon as that first gallon was gone, it was replaced by another full gallon, so two gallons of milk again sat in our refrigerator. At dinnertime, we each had a full glass by our plates and we suspected nothing.

Butch, my oldest brother, took the first swallow of milk. He looked confused, but didn't say anything. Richard, my second oldest brother, took a gulp of milk and looked at my mother; I took a tiny taste and immediately knew, we had been tricked! Without giving us any warning, Mom had mixed the store-bought milk with the powdered milk, trying to pass it off as one hundred percent real milk. In our eyes, this was an unjust betrayal; the three older siblings started talking at once, complaining about the milk and being tricked; this was disgusting and why didn't she at least tell us ... My father finally shouted above the uproar, "All right, that's enough! Drink your milk and eat your dinner or go to your rooms!" And then he quietly added, "You need to be grateful for what you have. I worked hard to earn the money for this meal and your mother worked hard preparing it. No more complaining."

We sat quietly, not making eye contact with our parents or with each other and feeling like ungrateful brats. I stared at my plate while the uncomfortable silence grew. Bruce, who up to that point was only an observer of the unfolding drama, took his first sip of milk. He looked around the table, shrugged his shoulders and said, "I like it." The rest of us ate our pork chops. Not a drop of milk was left in any of our glasses.

Postscript:
The Burnette children continued to drink a mixture of real and powdered milk for several more months. Once their father became more stabilized in his new job, one hundred percent store-bought milk became the norm. They never returned to drinking unpasteurized, raw milk from their own cows, although until the day they each left home, they ate beef from Herefords their father raised.

RESILIENCE
Robert Grossman
Lock Haven, Pennsylvania
March 17 and 18, 1936

In 1926, my mother and father bought a ladies clothing store. They had no money and Uncle Jake, my mother's uncle, loaned them $2000. Uncle Jake was considered a "mench", a good guy always willing to help out. Many Jewish families in small Pennsylvania towns, including several of my uncles, owned stores and were helpful in getting others started in their own retail businesses. My parents were young, had a year-old baby (me) and were at a point where they needed to establish themselves financially. The store seemed to be the perfect way to support a young family. It was centrally located in Lock Haven, at 9 East Main Street, in the heart of the main street shopping area of our town, and already had a following of loyal customers. My father took $900 dollars of the $2000 loan and fully paid for the business.

Although my father left school in the seventh grade, he was a good business manager. My mother was talented at selling the clothing and accessories and the business grew. In 1934, my parents bought a house on Water Street. The back yard had a beautiful view of the west branch of the Susquehanna River and the mountains beyond it. Our house was about 700 feet from the river, which was wide and shallow, no more than three or four feet at its deepest. We could walk across it, although no one ever did. Open sewers and industrial flowed into the river and while the view was beautiful, the water itself was ugly and unhealthy.

The store did well until late 1929 when the stock market crashed hard and kicked off the Great Depression. Not only did sales at the store suffer but, like many others, my father had speculatively bought stocks on margin, borrowing money from the bank to pay for stocks that ended up worthless. The market crash of 1929 wiped him out, leaving him with a huge debt to the bank. Many others in the same predicament declared bankruptcy, but my father did not. Instead, he worked out a payment plan to pay the bank off in seven years, using the business as collateral. For the next seven years, my parents worked even harder, meeting each payment to the bank on schedule. Sales were not as good as before the crash, but somehow they were able to pay off the loan. In early 1936, they made their last payment to the bank and were enjoying their successful family business. I was ten years old and my brother was six. Our lives were fairly uncomplicated, centered around the store, school, our friends and extended family.

Our mother not only was known as co-owner of Grossman's dress shop, but also for having a pantry and ice box always full of good food. At a moment's notice, she could whip up a feast. My father was involved in community groups and was known as a civic leader in town. Life was also good for the town; the economy was slowly coming back and we had somewhat reached a state of equilibrium. That is, until it started raining a few days before St. Patrick's Day, 1936.

Not many people living in the town at that time could remember the big floods that had occurred there—there hadn't been a flood in Lock Haven for many years. There was a big flood in 1865 and the June 3, 1889 flood was reported to be the worst ever experienced in Pennsylvania. That record was soon to be broken, although the residents started their day not quite expecting it to be a record-breaking day. On St. Patrick's Day morning of 1936, the Lock Haven Express newspaper ran the headline on its front page, "Rainfall Swells River and Creek; Flood Threat Nil." The weather report below the headline stated, "Fair tomorrow, weatherman's promise as rain lets up after steady downpours; all roads open." (from the Williamsport Sun Gazette, "Great floods recalled", David Kagan, September 14, 2008.)

My brother and I went to school that morning as usual, but it wasn't long before we were sent home because the river was rising. My father stayed at the store. It never occurred to him to move any of the furniture or fixtures. Besides, the store was only 2000 square feet and one story; there was no place to move anything. My brother, mother and I looked out the windows to our back yard, watching the river creep closer to our house. During other heavy rains, we had seen the water get as close as three or four feet from our house, so no one was disturbed as the water came closer. My father came home from the store, we ate dinner and my brother and I soon went to bed as it continued to rain.

Around one or two in the morning, my mother came into our room and quietly woke us. She and my father had stayed awake to watch the water and it was coming much closer to the house. She urged us to quickly get dressed and told us that the river was coming close to our house, so we were going to her friend's house; her friend lived in the hill section of town and the water couldn't reach her house. My mother gathered food to take with us—even with a raging flood at our door, she was the courteous guest, bringing delicious dishes to share.

My parents were very calm and my brother and I perceived the event as a big adventure. Running through the rain and mud, we helped carry the food and our clothes to our new 1936 Buick. I sat in the back seat holding a large bowl of homemade applesauce. My brother sat next to me, also holding a special food treat. My mother's friend lived only about one and a half miles from our house, in a neighborhood that was known as the "hill section" and on much higher ground than our neighborhood. We drove east on Water Street, parallel to the river, then turned south, away from the river, to cross Main Street and then towards Church Street on our way to the hill section.

Unbeknownst to us, eighty percent of Lock Haven was under water. I'm not sure what my father was thinking, but he was driving toward the intersection of Church Street and Second Street, which was one of the lowest elevation points in Lock Haven. My father paused the car as he approached the intersection. Dark swirling water was moving rapidly through it and we had no way of knowing how deep it was. My father gunned his new Buick forward and we entered the water. We quickly found out how deep the water was—at least three feet and deep enough to stall out the car. So there we sat, gripping homemade applesauce and other homemade delights as we watched the dark water rush by on all sides of our car. My parents remained calm and my brother and I were still enjoying the adventure aspects of the experience. There was no discussion of leaving the car—no one in my family could swim, and given the current's strength, the water probably would have overtaken us anyway. On the left side of our car was an apartment building and on the right side, the side I was sitting on, was a two-story single-family house. I heard someone call out my father's name and looked up at the house to see a man leaning out an upper story window. It was Al Williamson. He shouted out, "Milton, the fire truck is on its way—don't worry!" Fortunately, Mr. Williamson had seen our plight and called the fire department.

We sat in the car for another twenty minutes, with the swirling water inching higher on the car. Water was slightly seeping into the car from below; my feet were starting to feel wet. The fire truck finally arrived. Its wheels were at least four feet off the ground and truck itself was extremely tall. My brother and I watched in amazement as the fire truck backed up towards the front of our car. A fireman, who actually was a friend of our family's, got out of the fire truck and holding a large chain that was connected to the truck, pushed his way through the moving water to hook the chain to our front bumper. We were soon pulled out of the current. The firemen towed us about a half-mile to the hill section of town. Our friends knew we had been stranded and they were waiting for us a few blocks from the base of the hill section where the fire truck had towed us--they knew where to go because in a small town, news travels fast. All of us were worn out from the experience. We were grateful to be at our friends' house and soon fell asleep.

The rain and floods continued the next day and then they finally tapered off. Once the flood waters receded, we were anxious to see what happened to our home and to the store. The water marks showed that our house had been flooded with five feet of water and most everything was destroyed. The store was complete destruction. All of the merchandise, all of the fixtures, everything was either covered in mud, or soaking wet and swept into a sodden corner. My father stood looking at what he had built, what he and my mother had worked so hard for in order to become debt free. There was nothing left except a horrible odor. I can only imagine what was going through his head at the time. The banker who had lent my father money in 1929, the loan my father had just paid off, walked into the store as my father stood there. He put his arm around my father's shoulders and said, "Don't worry, we can do it again. We will loan you the money to get back into business." My father agreed and within two months, the doors to the store were once again open. Three or four years after that, the landlord decided to tear down the old building made of sun-dried bricks and put up a more modern one. Grossman's dress shop thrived in the new building.

Again, my parents worked hard to pay off the new debt. They were successful and had the loan paid off within six years. My parents continued to operate and manage the shop until 1960. During that time, they survived a 1954 fire that started in J.C. Penny's and destroyed a large part of the retail section in town. They were able to move a lot of the merchandise and opened in a temporary location until the new building was built.

I bought the business from my parents in 1960 and operated it until 1978, when I sold it. Having lived through the flood of 1936, I redesigned the new store to have a mezzanine high above ground level, where we could store things in the event of another flood, which we hoped would never happen, but it did. Beginning on June 21, 1972, Hurricane Agnes created a flood even worse than the 1936 one. Damage was severe, not just in Lock Haven, but throughout the state. Grossman's dress shop was again covered in mud, but this time, due to accurate forecasting and a mezzanine, we only lost thirty percent of our inventory.

Postscript:
The 1936 river crest in Lock Haven was 31.35 feet, one foot over the 1889 flood crest, creating an all-new record. The 1972 flood

crest was 31.50 feet. After its "Flood Threat Nil" headline of March 17, 1936, the Lock Haven Express newspaper was not able to publish another edition until March 28 because of its flooded offices.

Bob Grossman served in Europe as a 19-year-old rifleman during WWII. He participated in the last days of the Battle of the Bulge. After the war, he graduated from the University of Pennsylvania and then made many updated improvements to Grossman's, including adding the Estee' Lauder line of cosmetics. After selling the shop, he embarked upon a successful real estate career in Vero Beach, Florida. Bob is now retired in Naples, Florida and enjoys golfing with his wife, and visiting with his friends and family.

GEORGE AND BOB
Paul Compton
Verden & LaCross, Oklahoma
1930

Ribbons of black top now flow in all directions, but if you look long enough, you will find a sandy red earth road with stretches of rub board created where rain runoff has exposed some sandstone, red earth and mixes with rich black top soil in the low areas. Not so many years age, all of the developed roads leading to Verden, Oklahoma looked like this. If you follow the right roads, you can find my birthplace.

You will pass by where a small store once stood, where gas was hand pumped into an overhead glass cylinder from which then filled the car or truck. Gallon markers on the glass cylinder told the buyer how much he was getting. You will pass by where the cotton gin ran day and night during cotton season. You will come to a "correction line"—a point where the north-south road offset by about one-sixteenth of a mile to the west before continuing due north-south. Another four miles and you'll see a small creek paralleling the west side of the road and then you would arrive at the spot. A small farm that was an Indian lease and had two Indian graves next to the house.

There are no buildings now, but there used to be a small house and a barn. It was on that site, on Easter morning, April 11, 1925 that I was born. I'm told that I was delivered by a neighbor lady, Mrs. O'Neal, and that my sister thought the Easter Bunny had brought me and asked, "Can we keep him?" A couple of days after my birth Dr. Jesse Little, M.D., of Minco, Oklahoma came to the farm to check me. After checking me and putting drops in my eyes, he pronounced me fit and healthy.

When I was about two years old, Dad bought our Home Place and we moved. It was 10 miles north and two miles west of Verden. I cannot imagine a better place to spend my formative years. This community was known as the Lacrosse area. One mile from our home was a two-room country school. Adjacent to the school was a small store and gas station. There were three homes—two Buchannan families and the Comptons were grouped in the area, their farms and ranches radiating from that point.

My sister Helen was known as "Dear." As I began to talk, I could not say Helen and called her "Dea", which evolved to "Dear" once people could understand me. Dear started school at Oak Hill, about one and a half miles from our house, soon after we moved to the Home Place. Two O'Neal kids who lived down the road also went to Oak Hill. They rode horses to school. My sister rode a Shetland pony named Cupie, who was known to be a little ornery, but I always marveled that Dear rode him well.

Dear's next horse was a big bay named George, which our parents bought for her to ride to the LaCross school. I was about five, not yet going to school. I liked to wait for Dear to come home from school. Sometimes I walked to the south entry road to our house, which was only an eighth of a mile. Dear would let me ride George the rest of the way home while she walked. One of the days that she let me ride, I decided to see how fast George could run. I kicked him into a lope, but that wasn't fast enough. I leaned forward and whipped him with the long leather reins and we were really moving!

We were headed to the barn that was just southwest of the house. There was a large cottonwood tree next to a well where we pumped water into an old truck gas tank with the top part cut off. The tank was filled with water for the dogs and chickens. George probably had enough of me whipping him, because as we headed for the barn, he made a quick turn for the tree. I couldn't stop him. He ran under the tree and a limb knocked me out of the saddle. I just missed hitting the old gas tank, still got wet from knocking up some water, and was pretty well covered in dust.

My mother and dad observed most of this and came running. After I was looked over for injuries and they were sure I wasn't hurt, Dad gave me a good spanking and a firm lecture about handling horses. It was not about me running George hard, but it was about me whipping him to make him run faster. As I grew older and had my own horses, Dad never let me wear spurs. I liked to imagine that I was wearing large Spanish rowels. After all, that's what the movie cowboys wore. They made a great noise as a cowboy walked on the wooden sidewalks, but I was never allowed to wear them. My dad always said, "Good horses don't need to be ridden with spurs. If you need spurs, this reflects on you. You have not trained your horse properly."

I had a second incident during my fifth year that has always stayed in my memory. This one not about a horse, but about my dog. My first dog was a large tan and white English bulldog named Bob. He was a great pet and companion and was very protective of me and all the family. He never bothered neighbors or anyone that he was familiar with. Neighbors and friends stopped by and if no one was home, Bob never made a move to bother them or prevent them from going any place about the hose or barns. But this was not true of how he acted around strangers.

Our front yard was enclosed by a picket fence. Early one morning my mother was cutting weeds outside the fence and

I was playing nearby with toy trucks and Bob. All of a sudden, Bob growled and sprang to his feet, positioning himself between me and a hobo who suddenly appeared about twenty feet from us.

It was unusual to see strangers on our property. Our closest neighbor was more than a half mile away. Occasionally a stranger would come by, but riding horseback and looking for work. It was hard times and we always offered food for the stranger as well as something for his horse. All the neighbors did this. This man was on foot and must have walked down the creek, crossing the place on the southeast corner. This was a long way from the house. I suspect he saw my mother and had crossed a large field of corn that was growing between the creek and the house. At least, we had not observed his approach. He made no noise, nor had he called out from a distance as you would expect anyone to do. He was in dirty clothes, carrying a dirty and ragged bedroll. Bob stiffened and started a low growl as he slowly moved toward the stranger. The man immediately drew a large, open pocket knife, saying, "Call of your dog lady. Call off your dog!" My mother said softly to Bob, "Hold, hold!" Bob stood dead still, but continued to growl while maintaining eye contact with the man. My mother said, "Put away the knife—NOW! And get out of here!" The stranger quickly folded the knife, put it in his pocket and backed down the hill. After backing away for about 100 yards, he turned and ran down the road leading away from the house. Where the road crossed the creek, he dropped down inside its banks and disappeared. We never saw him again.

Postscript:
My mother told other neighbors about our experience with the stranger. None of them had seen anyone crossing their pastures or stopping to ask for food. I suspect the stranger was so frightened that he covered many miles that day to get away from the area. He was smart to be afraid of my mother and Bob. They made a formidable team.

DRIVING AT 12
Paul Compton
Verden & LaCross, Oklahoma
1937

When I was growing up, we had an earthen cellar in the hill adjacent to our house. In the fall of 1937, my parents decided to replace this cellar with a stone one.

Cellars were an important part of our lives in Oklahoma. They weren't just used as shelter from tornadoes, but were also our larder. Mother canned fruits, vegetables, and meat with a pressure cooker. These were stored in the cellar. Sweet and Irish potatoes and sometimes apples were wrapped and stored there. Also in the cellar was an incubator which held 50 eggs and was operated by a kerosene heater where we sometimes hatched baby chicks.

Mr. Gustafson, a stone mason from Chickasha, was hired to help my father build the new cellar. The stone was delivered by truck and then put in place by hand by Dad and Mr. Gustafson. This necessitated using tripods and pulleys to place the stones and cement to make them stay.

That same fall, we had just purchased a brand new two-door Chevrolet, the 1938 model which had just been released.

Although I was only twelve, I already knew how to drive a car and a truck, which wasn't unusual for country kids, but I hadn't had much experience driving by myself.

As Mr. Gustafson and my father worked, they ran out of cement. Dad decided that I should go after it. At twelve, I really wasn't very large but I thought I could do most anything any man could do and I was pretty excited to drive the new car by myself. Dad told me to be careful when I drove on the highway. It was 13 miles to Longbell Lumber in Pocasset—all of it dirt road except the last mile, Highway 81, which was paved. All went well. At Longbell, they loaded the trunk with sacks of cement. I don't recall how many sacks there were, but I do recall that each sack weighed 96 pounds and the car was loaded. I looked like a bootlegger with a full load.

I headed home, traversed the highway without a problem. But about two miles down the dirt road I had a flat, the first one ever on this car. I had picked up a nail in the lumber yard. The spare tire in the '38 Chevy was located in the floor of the trunk. All of the that cement had to come out to get to the spare. Then came the surprise. I thought I could do anything a man could do, but I could not reach in and lift a 96 pound sack of cement straight up and out of the trunk. There wasn't a house in sight and nobody was passing by.

After trying different ways of moving the cement sacks, I found that by rolling and then tumbling the sacks I was able to get the jack out, change the tire and then tumble the sacks back into the trunk. After a lot of hard work, I was on my way back home with the cement. Building the cellar was something I'll never forget.

Postscript:
The completion of the cellar added a new entity to Paul's daily life. Up to that point, he studied by the light of kerosene and Aladdin lamps. When the cellar was completed, a six-volt generator operating off a gasoline engine was added to it. The generator and engine were placed in the recessed escape area in

the back of the cellar so that it would vent well. His family's house was wired for six-volt lighting and the family enjoyed electrical lights.

Paul served as a pilot in the Army Air Corps from 1943 to 1945. After his service, he attended medical school at the University of Oklahoma and did general practice and surgery for seven years before returning to complete an additional residency in radiology. He practiced radiology in Tulsa, Oklahoma for 30 years. He is the grandfather of Scott Carter and has four other grandchildren. He resides in Tulsa where he also enjoys four great-grandchildren.

A MATTER OF PRINCIPLE
Ann Zimmerman Crane
Towson Maryland
1966

It's been more than 40 years but I remember the conversation as if it were yesterday. The year was 1966 and I was seated with my crowd of friends in the cafeteria of Dumbarton Junior High School in Towson, Maryland. As we ate sandwiches wrapped in wax paper and washed them down with ten cent cartons of milk, we chattered about this and that—what band was playing at Teen Center that week, who among us was going, and what we were going to wear. Someone mentioned that Beverly Thompson was running for Secretary in the upcoming Student Council elections.

Dreamboat Jimmy, who was sitting across the table from me, piped up, "Well that's fine for her to run for Secretary, but girls shouldn't run for President."

"Why not?" I asked in surprise.

"They just shouldn't, is all," he replied matter of factly. "Nobody would vote for them anyway."

I scanned the crowd for a reaction to his statement, but all I could see were blank stares. "Well, I'm going to run for President," I heard myself say defiantly.

Interest at the table picked up. All eyes were on Jimmy and me.

"I'll vote for you, Zimmerfleur," said Jeanne, a friend of mine from French class and the most popular girl in the group. Jimmy, who had a crush on Jeanne, looked miffed. And I, who had a crush on Jimmy, wondered what I had just gotten myself into. "Thanks, Jeanne," I said.

The bell rang, signaling three minutes until class started. As I hurried to my next class I thought, "Now all I have to do is win."

That evening I shared the news with Mom and Dad as we sat around the dinner table.

"I'm sure you'd make a very good Student Council President," Mom said. "But are you sure that's what you want to do?"

"What do you mean?" I asked surprised.

"Being a good president will take a lot of work," she observed as she began clearing the dishes from the table. "And I've never heard you mention an interest in Student Council before."

I paused for a moment, seeing her point. I actually thought Student Council was kind of dorky.

"I just can't let Jimmy get away with that," I said honestly. "Girls should be able to do the same things boys can."

"Just think about it some more before you commit yourself," she said. "You don't need to take on the injustices of the world at age fourteen. But if you really want to run, we'll help you in any way we can."

I could always count on Mom and Dad to be unendingly supportive. Mom was right—the boring demands of Student Council would likely be a major drag on my free time. But this was a matter of principle—something far more enduring than my after-school dalliances. I knew if I wasn't committed, both the principle and my social standing would suffer. That's when I decided to run and give it my all.

True to my mother's word, she took me to GC Murphy's 5 and 10 the next evening for campaign supplies. We left the store with 10 poster boards, some Magic Markers, several packages of construction paper, and several hundred little gold safety pins. Then, for a treat, we stopped at the soda fountain next door and ordered cherry Cokes.

As we sipped our drinks, we discussed my campaign. I decided on a flower theme featuring the same five-petal design that I doodled all over my notebooks. Mom suggested making flower-shaped campaign badges with "Ann for Pres" in the center.

I updated Mom on the official campaign status. "When I went to sign up for the election today," I began, "I saw only one other person signed up to run for President. His name is Bruce O'Hare. He's got a lot of friends, but he kind of looks like a mouse." I glanced sideways at Mom and could see she was trying not to look amused. "I'll just have to out-campaign him," I concluded.

"The key to your election is not the people that you know," she said, "but those you don't know. You'll need to introduce yourself to as many people as you can. You can do that by asking them to wear one of your flowers." Mom's father was a politician in Pennsylvania. Some of his tactics must have rubbed off.

"Is that what Papa does?" I asked.

"Let's just say that he's shaken a lot of hands in his day," she replied.

My best friend Karen came over the next day after school, to help me with the flowers. With glasses of Coke and a bag of cheese curls, we sat cross-legged on my bed and began cutting flowers out of colored paper. "Paint it Black" by the Rolling Stones played over and over again in the background.

After cutting the first 100 flowers, we took a break. From under my bed, I pulled a pack of Mom's Tareyton cigarettes. I offered one to Karen and took one for myself. After each rebellious puff, we carefully blew the smoke out the window. When we finished, we stubbed them out in an empty candy tin, which went back under the bed.

"Do you think I'm crazy to do this?" I asked as I picked up another stack of color paper.

"Maybe a little," she admitted. "I'd rather die than give a speech in front of the whole school."

"Ugh, I know. What am I going to wear?" I walked over to my closet and slid open the door. After pulling out half the contents of the closet, we agreed on a pink flowered skirt with a matching pink shell and a John Meyer mini-cable cardigan. I modeled the outfit and we both agreed that the pink complemented my dark brown hair and made me look older.

"What are you going to say in your speech?" Karen asked.

"That's a good question. I need a platform where I promise to do stuff, right?"

We threw around ideas, which I wrote on a sheet of lined paper from my notebook.

"I guess these should be things I can really do," I said as I looked at the list. "Free sodas at lunch—can't do that. Longer lunch breaks—don't think they'd go for that. Live bands at school dances—that's a possibility. We could charge a small admission to pay for the band. What do you think?"

"I like it!" Karen enthused. "The dances now are pretty lame. With a band, lots of kids would come just to hear the music."

"OK. That's my platform," I decided. Feeling more confident, I went back to cutting out flowers with renewed vigor.

The next day, I arrived at school early with my 10 posters and a bag full of flower badges. As I placed the posters strategically throughout the school, I noticed Bruce O'Hare and some of the other candidates doing the same. I looked at Bruce's posters with interest and was glad to see they contained only a rapidly scrawled "Bruce O'Hare for

President." Typical boy, I thought. Next to my neatly lettered, flower-bedecked posters, there was no contest.

After all the posters were hung, I made my way to the front doors and waited for the buses to arrive. As the first kids started pouring in, I confidently approached a girl I didn't know and said, "Good morning. I'm Ann Zimmerman and I'm running for Student Council President. Would you be willing to wear one of my flowers?"

The girl, who was obviously a seventh grader, looked flustered. "Here. Let me pin it to your shirt," I volunteered. She didn't object as I pinned on the flower. After thanking her, I walked up to another student—a boy this time—and repeated my routine. He, too, let me fasten a flower to his shirt.

By the time all the buses had arrived, I had pinned almost 50 students. As I hurried off to beat the bell for homeroom, a girl came running up to me and asked if she could have a flower. With a big smile, I handed her a flower and safety pin.

The two-week campaign flew by in a flurry of paper flowers. Over the weekend, I wrote my speech. I made it upbeat and funny and played up the benefits of bands at school dances. I then committed the speech to memory and practiced it every chance I got. Mom and Dad patiently listened and gave me tips on delivery. "Make eye contact with the audience," my father said. "Put some personality in your voice," my mother said. "Smile!" they both said.

The speeches were on Thursday and the election on Friday. On Wednesday, Bruce came up to my table in the cafeteria to talk some trash. "I know at least a hundred people who will vote for me," he boasted. "No one wants to vote for a GIRL! And those flowers of yours are just sissy and stupid. I'm going to win so big that your name will be mud after this election." With dismay, I saw Jimmy briefly smile in agreement.

I stood up, unwilling to be intimidated, and was about to go on the offensive when Karen did it for me. "Pipe down, pip squeak!" she said. "You look more like Ann's little brother than her opponent." I reached over to Bruce and condescendingly patted the top of his head. "It's okay little Brucie." Jimmy let out a hearty laugh and Bruce walked away in a huff. I felt kind of bad about making fun of Bruce like that. But then, this was war!

At 9:30 a.m. on a crisp Thursday morning, I reported to the auditorium to set up for the speeches. Mr. Yingling, the vice principal, stood on the stage next to a row of folding chairs.

"Miss Zimmerman," he said in his deep voice. "You are right here," as he pointed to the chair closest to the podium, "Mr. O'Hare—next to her." I sat in my assigned seat and crossed my legs at the ankle, just as my mother had counseled me. I glanced at Bruce out of the corner of my eye and saw he was fidgeting nervously.

Finally at 9:50 a.m., the first students began filing into seats by homeroom. A sea of unfamiliar faces piled into the auditorium. I started feeling Bruce's nervousness. I desperately needed a friendly face, so I watched intently for Karen to come in and saw her sit in the fifth row. Then I saw Jeanne. They were both wearing paper flowers, as were many of the other kids in the audience. Then I saw Dreamboat Jimmy amble down the aisle looking as irresistible as ever. In that moment, I realized I was ruining any chance I ever had with him. That kiss during last winter's sledding party seemed a distant memory.

My daydream about Jimmy was interrupted by Mr. Yingling addressing the assembly. He led the Pledge of Allegiance and then reminded everyone to give their full and undivided attention to the candidates. Assuming I was first, I prepared to stand up. But instead, he started at the far end of the row, calling on Danny Potter, a candidate for Parliamentarian. To pass the time, I reran the speech in my head over and over.

Then I heard Mr. Yingling call my name. This was it. I stood up and walked to the podium as if in a dream. "Look at the audience," I heard my father say. "Speak with conviction," I heard my mother say. "Smile!" they said in unison. I looked up out at the sea of faces, and my heart started to pound. "Find Karen," I commanded myself. I found her smiling face and it steadied me.

"I'm pleased and honored to speak to you today and ask for your vote for Student Council President." I heard the familiar words ring out through the microphone, strong and sure. Then I hit my groove. I could feel my eyes sparkle and my voice emote. I felt playful and powerful all at once, as the words came pouring out. My jokes elicited laughter and I realized I had the audience where I wanted them. Before I knew it, I heard myself thank the audience, flash a big smile, and sit down.

Mr. Yingling concluded the assembly by reminding everyone to vote. Then row by row, the kids began filing out. After collecting myself for a moment backstage, I emerged into the crowded hallway and headed to third period French class. As I walked in the room, Madame Salzmann said, "Votre discours était trés bon, mademoiselle Ann!"

"Trés bon, Zimmerfleur!" echoed Barbara, my French partner, as I sat down. The class laughed and I settled down to conjugate some verbs.

Voting took place in homeroom the next morning. Mrs. Baker passed out the ballots, instructing everyone to fold them twice after marking their choices. She then collected the ballots in a shoe box, taped on the lid, and delivered them to the office to be counted. In the announcements that morning, Mr. Yingling said that the results would be announced after lunch.

The morning dragged on forever. I was a bundle of nerves and left most of my lunch untouched. "What if I lose?" I asked myself, "Would that make Jimmy right?" Thoughts of self-doubt danced around my head—taunting me and my principles.

I was unsuccessfully trying to concentrate on fifth period math class when the loudspeaker crackled on. Mr. Yingling's voice boomed, "I am pleased to announce the winners of our

Student Council election. Our President next year will be Ann Zimmerman." The class erupted into applause and I sighed with relief. I couldn't wait to tell Mom and Dad!

In the hall after class, my friends clustered around to congratulate me. As the hubbub died down, I looked up to see Jimmy standing in front of me, smiling. My heart skipped a beat.

"I voted for you, you know," he said "And I think you'll make a really cool President."

Postscript:
Ann enjoyed her term as student council president and continued to assert her prerogative to venture into traditionally male-dominated domains by becoming one of the University of Maryland's pioneering female Electrical Engineering graduates in 1975.

INDEPENDENCE
Margy Kesler
1934
Barnes, Wisconsin

As a fourteen-year-old schoolgirl, I moved into a cabin with three other girls my age with no adult present, and there I stayed for most of the next four years. The events leading up to my young independence weren't unusual for that time and place, but for me, it created memories and friendships that I will never forget.

My education until mid-seventh grade was in the southern part of Wisconsin. When I was 12, my family moved to the community of Barnes, in northern Wisconsin, where I finished seventh and eighth grades in a one-room school. Barnes had seven elementary schools, spaced just a few miles apart. My school only had about 15 children that ranged from six years old to 14. Even with the wide range in ages, we all got along well and there were no problems with us all learning in the same room. The high school was in the small town of Drummond, about 15 miles from Barnes. There was a school bus from Barnes to Drummond, but it only stopped on the main routes. The closest bus stop from our house was three miles, not quite close enough to our house to walk.

My parents had made friends with an elderly couple who lived not far away. My father had helped out on their farm and they had helped on ours. My mother was in the Ladies' Aid Society with the elderly woman. The older couple's house was right on the bus route and they had a cabin on their property. My parents worked out an arrangement with the couple for me and three other girls to live in the cabin during the school week. The older couple would check in on us and we would be close to the bus stop.

I was eager to go to high school. I very much wanted to be a secretary and hoped to attend a business school that would prepare me for that profession. I could see myself efficiently taking notes, accurately putting neat numbers in a ledger book and crisply running the clerical duties of an office. This was an enormously exciting step for me—not only would I be attending high school classes, but I would be living in a cabin with other girls and being more independent than I had ever been in my life. While I knew the three other girls who would be staying in the cabin with me, we weren't particularly close friends. That changed very quickly; we all became very close and one of them became a life-long dear friend.

What to wear my first day of high school was somewhat of a dilemma. My dresses all looked fine for a one-room elementary school, but didn't quite have the style I felt I needed for high school's first day. My mother very much understood my concern. She also knew that I absolutely loved her soft green dress that had a coordinating green and tan jacket. It was always my favorite. Although my mother loved that dress and enjoyed wearing it, she unselfishly offered to cut it down and make it fit me. When I pulled the dress on after my mother finished the alterations, I felt very grown up and very dressed up, almost like a secretary. I was ready for high school.

My father and mother drove me to the cabin the weekend before the first week of school. I had already met the elderly couple and my cabin-mates. All of our parents sent plenty of food to see us through the week. We were farm kids and ate lots of potatoes, homemade bread, homemade cookies and cakes and our parents made sure we had ample amounts. There was no refrigerator; we brought meat that would keep at least two days. We put away the food, put away our things and busily chatted about what our first week might be like as our parents made their farewells and left.

The next morning we all walked the short distance to the bus stop. I had on my "new" green dress and my cabin-mates also had on special dresses. There were other students waiting at the stop, some upper classmen. We saw the bus make its approach and slowly stop where we stood. The bus was really a truck. It had a wooden box built onto the truck bed. We stepped on a wooden step and went through the entryway. The bus driver closed the entryway door and locked it from the outside. There was no heat in the bus-box, just some exhaust that would make its way in. Amazingly, none of us were made the worse for the four years we each rode in that vehicle. Our ride was about 15 miles to the high school. We made it fun—we sang, told jokes and laughed lots.

When we entered our ninth grade classroom on that first day, we knew we were seen as different. The ninth graders from Drummond all knew each other, had grown up with each other in the town. We were outsiders from the farms. I sort of had anticipated that, but hadn't let it worry me too much, and it was a good thing because it would have been needless worry. The Drummond students were all friendly and welcoming. It didn't take too long to realize that the town kids were a good bunch and were happy to see new faces.

In my four years of high school, I took all of the mathematics classes available. I also took stenography, book keeping and business classes. I selected classes that would help me become a secretary. I worked hard and made good grades.

We fell into a routine at the cabin. We prepared our dinner together from the food our parents had sent with us, and we studied together. The elderly couple visited often, I think more for company than to check on us. Our parents picked us up from the cabin every Friday and we enjoyed weekends with our families at home. On Sunday night, my father drove me back to the cabin. If snow had fallen, he hitched the horses up to our sleigh, complete with sleigh bells. I loved those snowy Sundays, going back to the cabin in the sleigh, listening to the bells and moving over the beautiful snow.

When we started our second year in the cabin, two of the girls in the cabin who were sisters had a brother starting ninth grade. He moved into the big farmhouse with the couple, but ate dinner and studied with us. My third year, a second brother joined the first in the farmhouse and also ate and studied with us in the cabin. There were always four girls in the cabin. When one graduated and moved out, another would take her place.

When I finally graduated, I was ready to fulfill my dream of becoming a secretary. There was a school, Kate Bartley's Business School in Superior City, that I wanted to attend. I had been offered a scholarship to go to Teacher's College, but my heart was on secretarial school. My parents took me to Kate Bartley's Business School to visit and ask questions. The school was adamant that all money had to be paid up front. We didn't have that kind of money. It was during the depression and I'm not sure if anyone could afford the school. I left feeling very down, but wasn't ready to give up my goal.

After the disappointment of not being able to pay for Kate Bartley's, I ended up going to Teachers' College on the scholarship. I finished my two-year program, received my teaching certification and took a job teaching first through eighth graders in a one-room schoolhouse. I loved the children, loved watching them grow and learn and very much enjoyed my first year of teaching. I hadn't given up my dream of being a secretary. That spring, I was offered and accepted a stenographer's position as a summer job. After two summers of sitting in a small stuffy office, taking and transcribing someone else's words, I realized that being a secretary wasn't for me. My real joy was in the classroom. I couldn't imagine not teaching children. After the second summer of being a stenographer, I returned to my classroom with the intent to stay for good. My mother was overjoyed. She had always wanted to be a teacher but had married young and had to raise children and work on the farm. It was like she was finally seeing her personal wish come true.

I never regretted selecting teaching over a secretarial career. For me, the joy and rewards were far greater than anything I would have gained from a secretarial career. Sometimes things just work out right.

Postscript:
Mrs. Kesler taught school for more than 29 years. She took a 16 year break to raise her sons and help her husband with the family service station. At 93 years of age, Mrs. Kesler still lives in Wisconsin and enjoys her church, her family and friends, and a darn good fish fry.

WATER CONSERVATION FIFTIES-FARM STYLE
Margaret Speke Davison
Moville, Iowa
The 1950s and Early 1960s

I was born in 1950 and grew up on my family's third generation farm in northwest Iowa. For some reason, I'm either cursed or blessed with a very keen memory mechanism that triggers with a growing frequency and my memories of those years keep growing. One area of vivid memories that often plays in my head centers around that precious, simple commodity—water.

Water was very dear on the farm and we had to conserve it carefully. No water went to waste. Like other farm families in our community, we conserved because of the limitations of our water sources, which were a well with an electric windmill and a cistern, as well as the limitations of our waste water disposal system, which was a septic system that could only handle so much water at one time. Use of the well and septic impacted our daily routine in ways that urban and suburban dwellers did not experience.

Not even one extra drop of water was allowed to go to waste. There was always a red plastic basin in the tub to catch any extra water that would go to good use. As kids, we were barefoot much of the time and our feet usually picked up dirt, mud, or purple mulberry stains from our yard. The red plastic basin was just the right size for our feet. On warm summer nights, after a day of playing in the yard, Mom or Dad would add a small ration of warm water to the basin. We took turns sitting on the back porch bench with our feet in the basin and a bar of Lava soap nearby for scrubbing the dirt and the stains from between our toes and the bottoms of our feet. Mom kept a stack of slightly worn, but very clean, towels folded neatly nearby for drying.

Our other bathing would be in our tub, once a week. Although it is stereotypical of the "rural rubes taking their weekly Saturday night bath", it was authentic for us. One of our parents turned on the bathtub faucet, filling only the smallest layer of water, which just covered the tub floor. Our eldest sister, Judy, took her bath first, then Mary, the middle sister, bathed next in the same water, and then my bath was always the last, with an ever-so-slight warm up of hot water from the faucet. In later years I realized what a remarkable real-life story those baths made and why they elicited responses of "No way!" and guffaws from my contemporaries.

When I was eleven, I took the train to Denver by myself with money I saved from washing the farm eggs. My Aunt Beryl and her husband Bill lived quite the sophisticated city life in an apartment there. My first night there, my aunt "drew a bath" (a term new to me). When I went into the bathroom to take my bath, I froze in shocked horror. The tub was full to the top! I climbed in carefully for fear of slipping under the water, took my bath, and when finished, I just could not pull the plug on all that hot clean water (relatively speaking). So, of course, I called out to my aunt and uncle asking who would like to take the next bath. There was absolutely no response from them. I chuckle to this day, with a bit of a red face, about the amused looks they must have given each other, although my aunt had grown up on that very same farm during the hard times.

Bath time wasn't the only time we saved water. With the goal of conserving every possible drop, my mother had a system of doing the wash (pronounced "warsh" in Iowan vernacular) so as to get as much out of one washer full of water as she could. She'd sort all the clothes into the various categories and prioritized each pile, from the whites which were the most important to do in clean soapy water, to the last load, which contained my dad's overalls and shirts that he wore while he working in the field. She was a fastidious woman in every way and her laundry standards were also high. It wasn't easy work. She had to be alert and ready to catch each load at the exact end of the wash cycle, before the water started draining out automatically as the machine went into the spin cycle. Using her wooden laundry stick, she fished out each piece of clothing, placed it into the tub next to the washer, put the next load in, added soap only if needed, turned the dial around to begin the washing again, and repeated these steps until each load had used the same water. When it was time for the rinse cycle of each load, she went through the same arduous process again. My mother was a "green" practitioner before the word was even coined. And despite a pretty significant thyroid fatigue condition, she was ready and willing to do what it took to save water and economize. Of course, her three daughters were all taught to do the laundry using her procedure.

Postscript:
When Margaret left home and lived on her own, she took great pleasure in being able to do laundry the "normal" way. Today she is very conservation-minded and as a reminder, keeps her mother's old cherished wood laundry stick in her laundry room.

LEADER OF THE BAND
Margaret Speke Davison
Woodbury Central High School
Moville and Climbing Hill, Iowa
1968

I was first chair clarinet in my high school concert band. It was an honored position, but in my senior year, I aimed higher—I wanted to become the drum majorette, leader of the entire band. The opportunity arose when our band teacher raised the bar for the first time in the history of our school band; he decided enough with the best baton twirler leading the band, it should be a member of the band.

I concurred heartily with dismissing the baton twirler, because I'd admired and studied the high-profile drum majorettes on television as they led their huge collegiate bands while strutting their stuff in parades and halftime shows. Some even climbed ladders to direct the music as the band played and marched in complicated formations. I just knew I was perfect for the part and spent many hours practicing and imagining myself as leader of our band. My audition was an actual march down Main Street. I had a vision of how the drum major should perform fixed in my mind and I didn't disappoint myself when I pranced the goose-step crossing back and forth diagonally while raising high that giant pointed baton. I was grand, but only in my own delusional mind's eye. As it turned out, I succeeded only at being comical to everyone else. As usual I went too big. However, always loving an audience, I did enjoy the fact that I cracked up my band mates so much that they could barely play their music as they marched along Main Street that day.

But alas, since drum majorette didn't pan out, I had to settle for marching band cymbalist and grew into that loud and high profile role quite happily—until a day that still lives in personal infamy for me. It was a warm autumn day when our band took the school bus to Buena Vista College's Homecoming to perform in the home-coming parade down the streets of Storm Lake. The bus was loaded with band students, music instruments, and the school-owned percussion pieces which were haphazardly tossed into the back of the bus.

I had even more baggage along with me. The football game the night prior had been bone-chilling and my friend, Susan, had kindly lent me mittens that her mother had knit for her. The mittens kept my hands warm when not cheer leading out in front of the crowd. I'd forgotten to give them back at the end of the night, so I stuffed them into the trousers of my band uniform and brought them along the next morning. Once in Storm Lake, we all piled off the bus and quickly got ready to line up for the parade. Earlier, unbeknownst to me, when I'd retrieved the cymbals in the back of the bus, one of the thick circular lamb's wool hand protectors had disappeared. Realizing this when we hurriedly lined up, I knew I didn't have time to go back and search for it, and I also knew that my hand would be badly cut and in pain if I didn't have protection. Our band instructor was quite strict and had firm rules about how we needed to keep in straight lines and NEVER break ranks. So the only thing I could do to quickly solve the problem was to use my friend's mitten to serve as protector, which luckily was flesh colored and still in my uniform pocket. Off we went, marching along just fine. Then right in the middle of the main part of the parade where the crowd was thickest and we needed to be our very best, the problematic cymbal completely broke off the leather strap and went rolling down the street. It seemed that the leather strap which held it all together was loosened when the lamb's wool pad came off. Time sped up and reality morphed for me as the huge mishap progressed. I had to break ranks to run after the cymbal because I didn't want to face our persnickety teacher upon the loss of an expensive school instrument. Imagine a girl, in uniform, white shiny tall hat with white plume atop bobbing along, chasing a cymbal. This was beyond my love of an audience, my love of playing the clown just for a laugh. This was seriously embarrassing.

When the cymbal finally slowed, taking its sweet time to spin to a final stop while I watched. I grabbed at it frantically. However, I couldn't grasp the cymbal because I had on my friend's mitten. Off came the mitten and up came the cymbal, but now what? I simply had no choice but to run Pall Mall between other schools' bands, with the crowd watching, to get back into line, with you-know-who glowering as he marched alongside our band. Now, face fully flushed red hot, I got back into rank and marched holding the cymbals over both arms and hands as if I were delivering a large pizza, with the mitten placed on top. I was so flustered all I wanted was to have this nightmare over with. But nooooo, I was still the subject of God's little practical joke. Somehow, the mitten slipped off the shiny surface of the useless cymbals. At this point, I would've let the mitten go with no compunction about losing the darn thing. But it was borrowed, handmade by Susan's mother and I had to do what was right. So, breaking ranks once again, I ran back to pick up the mitten, and turned to chase after my band a second time. Ironically, my friend Susan was the person who beat me out of the position of drum majorette. During the parade, she was up front, strutting her stuff, with no idea of the drama her mitten was creating.

Later that year, for my school newspaper's senior interview, when asked my most embarrassing moment in life, it took me no time to answer. Chasing that cymbal, and then chasing my friend's hand-knitted mitten, still rates as one of my life's most embarrassing moments.

Postscript:
Although Margaret was trained as a classical pianist from early childhood through college, she decided not to follow a career in music. She still loves an audience and making people laugh. She took tap dancing and singing lessons in order to win a spot in the chorus line of the Des Moines' Community Theater production of "42nd Street". Margaret helped develop a 15-year grassroots educational friendship program between her community in Urbandale, Iowa and Item, Nigeria (in Biafra) and traveled to the village five times. Currently, Margaret occasionally writes articles for the "Thoughts of Home" column in the Moville Record newspaper and finds ways to make her granddaughter heartily laugh.

THE MANGO KID
Hank Fowler
Panama
1954

My father was stationed at Howard Air Force Base in the Panama Canal Zone for two years. Dad was a staff sergeant in the United States Air Force. We lived on base and our housing complex consisted of three-story apartment buildings that had four units on each level, so 12 families to a building. In our complex, there were six of these buildings that surrounded a playground area. An added bonus for the kids who lived there was a mango tree grove that grew between the building we lived in and the one next door. The base housing was a great place for us kids—it was safe, fun and there were lots of adults around who knew us all and kept us out of trouble. As a four-year-old, I was independent and played outside without worrying my parents. My favorite place to play was under the mango trees. I loved to eat mangos.

Denny, my older brother, was six years older than me. As a ten-year-old, he didn't have too much time for his kid brother. Denny and his friends were very adept at climbing the mango trees, picking the best mangos, and throwing them down to eat as soon as they climbed out of the tree. I was way too small to climb the tree, but I often watched Denny and his friends climb and I always asked them to give me a mango. Sometimes they gave me one, but usually they ignored me.

When mangos become over-ripened, they fall to the ground and those were the mangos I ate. Most of the time they were pretty mushy and just on the verge of spoiled, but I ate them anyway. A mango's skin is very tough and of course I didn't have a knife. My solution was to bite through the skin to get to the fruit—it made a mess, all over my face, hair, hands and my shirt and shorts. My mother chastised me when I went back to our apartment with juice all over my face and clothes. She was afraid that eating mangos off of the ground would make me sick. I always agreeably acknowledged her instruction, but then I managed to forget.

One time when I returned from a mango feast, my dad had just gotten home from work. He was very much a military father, hard on discipline and expecting obedience and order from his sons. My mother took one look at me, and immediately starting telling me how much trouble I was in for disobeying and eating the mangos off of the ground. She didn't have to tell me. I knew I was in trouble and with my father home, it could only get worse. In my most innocent voice and with my most angelic expression, I told my parents I had not eaten any mangos. My mother looked at me and said, "Will you then tell me why there is mango all over your face and clothes? The juice is still dripping down your chin." I had no answer. I just stood there looking from my mom to my dad, preparing myself for punishment. Finally, Dad looked at me and said, "Well, maybe he's just the mango kid." The name stuck, and I was careful to try to only pick up the least mushy mangos to eat after that. They never did make me sick.

My sweet tooth went beyond mangos. I also loved cookies. My mom was pretty good at supplying us with plenty of baked goods, but I really loved cookies. Although I was well fed, I was a skinny four-year-old. I was average height, but had a light-bulb head that accentuated my skinniness. To make me look even more like a third-world orphan, Dad kept my hair (and that of my brothers) shaved close to our heads in good military style. I ate plenty at home, but was always hungry, especially for cookies.

I knew most of the families in our apartment complex and was allowed to play outside as long as I stayed within the area that surrounded our playground. Most of the families had a Panamanian maid and most of the mothers stayed at home. I knew which families had mothers and maids who baked and also which ones were a soft touch. I perfected a routine that scored more cookies than any other kid in the complex. I would knock on the door of one of soft touches, put a sorry and pathetic look on my face and then say, "I'm so hungry—do you have any cookies for me to eat?" I usually knocked on three or four doors and was pretty successful at getting a cookie or two from each door. But as with the mangos, I wasn't good at hiding the evidence. I always seemed to show up at home with chocolate smeared across my face or cookie crumbs down my shirt. Mom was aghast. She feared the neighbors thought she was starving me. She told me to stop begging for cookies and told the neighbors to not to feed me, but I still knocked and they still gave me cookies. Mom never dissuaded me from mooching off the neighbors or eating spoiled mangos off the ground.

Postscript:
Howard Air Force Base was turned over to Panama in 1999 as a part of the Torrijos-Carter Treaties. According to Wikipedia, much of the former base is now used for technology companies' call centers, most notably Dell Computers. The Fowler family continued their military moves until their father, Warren Henry Fowler, Jr., retired in 1968.

HOT BEANS
Hank Fowler
Kyushu, Japan
1964

For three years, my dad was stationed at Itazuke Air Force Base on the southern island of Kyushu. My family lived off-base in a local Japanese neighborhood with a few other military families mixed in with Japanese families. I had joined a Boy Scout troop and discovered that I loved to hike the nearby mountains. My favorite mountain was "Monkey Mountain." I don't know if Monkey Mountain was the English translation of the Japanese name, or if the mountain's real name just sounded like "monkey". It was an hour's walk from our house to the foot of the mountain. From the base to the top was about 1000 feet and it took me two hours to get to the summit.

One Saturday morning when I was 13, I decided to hike up Monkey Mountain. My usual hiking buddy, Hiroshi, was in school because Japanese kids had to go to school six days a week. I didn't want to wait until Sunday, when Hiroshi could go with me. But my mom didn't want me to go alone, so told me to take my younger brother, Jeff, who was 11 at the time.

Jeff was pretty excited to tag along, although I wasn't so excited to have his company. I made him pack up our food—hot dogs, buns and a can of Campbell's Pork 'n Beans.

We took off, well equipped with our food, matches for the fire to cook the hotdogs and my scout knife in my knapsack. The hike up was fun, with just the right of amount of challenges for two boys. We followed the trails up, sometimes climbing over rocks and pulling ourselves up on the steep slopes. When we reached the top, we went to my usual camping spot. It had a view of the valley below and we felt like we were on top of the world. We were hungry, so I built a fire, the way I'd learned in Boy Scouts, digging a pit and encircling it with rocks. Without realizing it, I put too much wood in the pit, some of it right up to the rocks. After lighting the fire, we started pulling out our food. I found sticks to roast the hot dogs and sharpened the ends with my knife.

Just as I was about to put the hot dogs on the sticks, Jeff asked, "Where's the can opener for the beans?" My answer was, "Well you packed the food, where'd you put it?" The can opener was clearly missing and I blamed Jeff. I figured I could still heat up the beans in the can. I'd just punch holes in the top with my Scout knife to release the steam and once they were hot, use the knife to open the can enough to spill out the beans. I put the can down on the rocks next to the fire and forgot about it. But before I went to get my knife, we started roasting our hot dogs.

Our campfire was growing huge and hot so we pulled the hot dogs out after only a few minutes. The hot dogs smelled great, so we put them in the buns and sat next to the fire to eat. With some food in my stomach, I started feeling a little more forgiving toward Jeff. All of sudden, there was a huge explosion that made both of us jump. The can of beans had over-heated up on the hot rocks and blew apart. Jeff and I were sitting so close to it, we were both splattered with hot beans and sauce. The beans burned our faces and dotted our shirts. We quickly wiped away the beans; both of us had a few small blisters where the hottest beans burned our skin. We were lucky we weren't hit by any sharp pieces from the exploded can. I picked up what was left of the can. "Hey, there are some beans left in here. We didn't need the can opener after all!" We sat back down and enjoyed the hot dogs and what was left of the beans. Needless to say, Mom never knew about the exploding bean can.

Postscript:
All four of the Fowler boys served their country in the Armed Forces, following in the tradition of their father and grandfather. Hank (Warren Henry Fowler III) retired from the Army after 28 years of service. He then worked for the Defense Intelligence Agency (DIA). Between his Army and DIA careers, Hank has been deployed to Cambodia, Thailand, Bosnia, Kosovo, Afghanistan, and Iraq. Maybe that exploding bean can was getting him ready for something.

ROBERT THE ROBOT
Kris Wells
1954
El Paso, Texas

I was convinced that if I could get Robert the Robot for Christmas, my dreaded room cleaning burden would be lifted and "Robbie" would zip around the room at my command, picking up all my kid debris and neatly depositing all in the much-dented toy-box. My kid dreams of effortless "cleanup your room" possibilities prompted a campaign not subsequently equaled until the great BB gun siege of 1957. Robbie was going to be the perfect clean-up-my-room machine and at six, I knew my life would change if I could only get a Robert the Robot. In fairness, just check out the box ...

IT'S FUN! YOU MAKE HIM WALK! YOU MAKE HIM TALK! YOU STEER HIM TOO! And Robbie's HANDS CLASP OBJECTS! On the box I could see real toys in Robbie's mechanical hands as he lumbered around some lucky kid's room, picking up stuff and dutifully hauling it to the lucky kid's toy-box. The picture showed me in my imagined future (except for the freckles) and Robbie beaming with real electricity as he tended to his responsibilities. Clearly, Robbie would walk around cleaning my room and I could just sit back and send him on the way. But wait, there's more! SENSATIONAL NEW, PATENTED TALKING* DEVICE!

I didn't know what that asterisk meant in those days but figured it had to be something even better since it was extra. Like the exclamation point after the DEVICE! If I could just persuade Mom and Dad that Robbie is what I really, really, really, wanted for Christmas they would get it for me (none of that Santa stuff for a sophisticated fellow like me.) I was relentless and they caved.

I don't remember the moment when I first opened the box and discovered that Robbie was made of plastic, but it left a mark. I'm sure there was some acting involved because the great event was attended by Mom and Dad. Any hesitation or lack of enthusiasm on my part would not have bode well for future "things I want for Christmas" campaigns. Like I said, it had been a long and determined effort that led to my success that morning. Apparently Ideal Toy Co. product number 4049 was very popular indeed and required advanced parental foraging to secure the prize. I'd better like it.

Well, more detailed examination first revealed that Robert was not nearly as talkative as I had imagined. You could turn a handle on his back and a tiny plastic disc would play, "I am Robert, mechanical man. Drive me and steer wherever you can." But that's all he said. Ever. Faster or slower, it was always the same.

Indeed it seemed a useless feature, except for its soon discovered ability to separate the syllables of "Ro" and "bot." Then in response to my carefully timed and repeatedly practiced quarter-turn of the handle, Robbie would blurt out, "buhtt!" which was hilarious at the time.

Okay, so the talking part was a bit disappointing, I didn't really care that much. That wasn't what I saw as Robbie's principal responsibility.

Stubbornly, I attacked the wrapping-paper, ribbon, and toy-laden Christmas morning floor to carefully fit things into Robbie's largely useless claws and direct him with the impossibly difficult-to-comprehend "EASY TO OPERATE REMOTE CONTROL!" Getting stuff to remain affixed to his rudimentary plastic clamps while I "steered" Robbie turned out to be an early lesson in composure maintenance. And yet I kept a happy face on this disconcerting state of affairs.

Robert the Robot inside the box was very different from Robert on the outside. In desperation, and under the watchful eyes of Mom and Dad, I began to see that it would be easier to clean up my room without Robbie's assistance. Months of careful maneuvering to secure this Christmas prize began to assume a pale significance.

Even with Robbie's abruptly discovered and admittedly disappointing limitations, he was a really cool toy, and like all toys mixed with younger brothers, Robbie was worth fighting over.

Ultimately, some of his parts were removed to support other projects. In the ensuing years, he lost his head to a squabble with my little brother—but Mom tirelessly pursued a replacement and fixed it. Robbie gained a decal or two left over from various model airplane construction projects and his clampy hands were damaged sometime. The cool D-Cell battery-powered flashlight bulb gizmo on his new head became a component in my later construction of a working fly guillotine.

Postscript:
The lessons learned from Robert the Robot did not stick. Kris had yet another mail order experience a couple of years later—read on.

MONKEY IN A TEACUP
Kris Wells
1959
Upstate New York

My friend Danny lived in a big house with his Mom and hundreds of comic books, the remains of a divorce that left only-child Danny without a dad. The comic books substituted and we spent hours reading The Green Lantern, The Phantom, The Green Arrow and other crime-fighting denizens of Danny's upstairs bedroom, ignoring more pedestrian heroes like Superman and Batman. We thought comics like Archie and Classics Illustrated were boring. Danny's comic books were stacked tall in his closet and spilled out onto his bedroom floor, where we would pass the hours in imaginary worlds of good guys blowing up bad guys in spectacular ways. I was always especially attentive to the wonderful stuff that could be mail-ordered off the comics' back pages.

Amongst the enticements were all manner of ways to improve your life for only a few cents. You could build an intimidating Charles Atlas body and thereby avoid having sand kicked in your face at the beach. You could purchase

"X-Ray Specs" that enabled you to see through girls' clothes. The one-dollar "Hypno-Coin," was a new "Pocket sized invention that helps hypnotize in minutes—guaranteed or your money back." Danny and I tried hypnotizing each other with regular coins but it didn't work.

I sent off for fake vomit, Sea Monkeys (just ADD WATER), and a "Black Eye Gag" that promised to give a black eye to anyone who dared peek into the mysterious-looking telescope device to see a naughty picture. I figured seeing a naughty picture was worth a black eye but after my four-dollar investment and weeks of waiting for the package, only the vomit was worth it. The Black Eye Gag turned out to be a cheesy little cardboard tube with black chalk on one end and nothing to see on the other. And the Sea Monkeys never emerged from their slowly evaporating plastic cup on my window shelf.

Despite my experience and disappointments, when I saw the offer of a tiny monkey in a teacup, it was just too irresistible. A monkey. Now there was a pet. I remember reading the comic book ad carefully but mostly I remember reading the word FREE several times. The rest was confusing, but I understood FREE and filled out the paperwork and mailed it off to Dean Studios in Des Moines, Iowa.

Every day I would come home from school hoping that my miniature monkey had been delivered. This was not something I had shared with Mom and Dad because I was unsure how they would react to having a monkey in the house, but I figured once I got him and got yelled at, I would still have the monkey. He was, after all, very small and I was sure he could live in my room and not disturb anybody. He could be like a good little brother instead of the ones I had.

The little monkey didn't come. Instead, the Post Office brought a big C.O.D. box of stuff that I was supposed to get the neighbors to buy. Mom refused it, my monkey remained in Des Moines, and I got in trouble. I learned again the hazards of mail order and that C.O.D. stood for "Cash on Delivery," but got off with just a lecture. Apparently, being duped by advertisements was not really criminal, just dumb. Nevertheless, I learned about reading the fine print and never sent off for anything else offered on the pages of a comic book. But a Whoopee Cushion would have been nice for when I went to high school ...

Postscript:
After discovering the perils of mail order, Kris went on to become an Air Force Colonel. He produced and directed film and television for the USAF. Since retirement, he has written and spoken on the history and technology of oil exploration and production in America.

A HOLE IN THE BUCKET
Nancy Burnette Fowler
1962
Swannanoa, N.C.

The summer after fifth grade was a fun one. I played softball with my brothers and cousins, went to Bible School, swam at the public pool, and had a crush on a boy named Weasel. As fun as the summer was, by late July, I was looking forward to seeing my school friends that I'd known since the first grade. I was also looking forward to having Mrs. Hipps as my teacher because she was known as one of the best teachers at Swannanoa Elementary. My sixth grade didn't turn out quite the way I thought it would. Not only did I have a different teacher for most of the year, but new children in my class ended up making my sixth grade classroom anything but what I expected.

Not too many weeks into the school year, we learned that Mrs. Hipps needed surgery and would be gone for a very long time. Mrs. "L." was going to be our substitute. From a likeability perspective, Mrs. L. was doomed. First and foremost, she was not Mrs. Hipps. Added to that, she was very thin, with an angular face that did not smile and piercing eyes that looked straight through children. These physical features were enough to curtail any warmth we might have felt toward Mrs. L., but there was even more. She only had one arm. The fact is, Mrs. L. could have been beautiful, talented, friendly, in possession of all her limbs, and we would not have liked her simply because she was not Mrs. Hipps. She never had a chance.

We were raised to be polite children who knew it was rude to stare. We had several adults and children in our midst with disabilities and we were very accepting of them. Mr. Green lost his arm in a work accident. My grandfather lost several fingers at his sawmill. My best friend had a cerebral palsied uncle and there were many other people with differences in our community. These were friends, neighbors and relatives that we grew up with. We were accustomed to them and knew when to help them and when to step back. But, we had never had a teacher with any type of disability. We couldn't help ourselves. We stared. Just past her left elbow, her arm ended in a stump wrapped in gauze. It was not just the missing arm that fascinated us; we also were amazed at her ability to adapt to its loss.

Mrs. L. had perfect blackboard handwriting. She wrote in small, precise letters with her one hand. But her handwriting wasn't the amazing part; the amazing part was when she made a mistake. She always held the blackboard eraser in the crook of her stump elbow as she wrote. When she needed the eraser, which was rare, she flipped it out of the crook of her arm and caught it with her hand. Almost simultaneously, she tossed the chalk and caught it in the crook of half-arm. From Mrs. L.'s first day on, we watched intently, hoping she would make a mistake so that we could watch the magic eraser-chalk exchange trick.

We soon fell into a routine, math and social studies in the morning while we were fresh, recess after lunch, spelling and English late afternoon. While we didn't love Mrs. L., we were making academic progress and the classroom was peaceful. That is, until our school routine was turned its side.

It was a rare occasion that new students came to Swannanoa Elementary, but about a month after Mrs. L. arrived, two new students joined our class. When Mrs. L. introduced "Paul" and "Pauline" to our class, we didn't know that we were about to learn a lesson that could never be found in a book. Paul and Pauline were brother and sister. Pauline was a year older and two heads taller than Paul; she had been held back a year and was clearly the leader of the two.

While we were all used to wearing hand-me-downs, ours were usually mended, mostly clean and within a size or two of fitting. Paul and Pauline's clothing passed our hand-me-down boundaries of acceptance. Both were pretty much wearing adult clothing that wasn't anywhere near fitting, but it didn't seem to bother either one of them. When introduced to the class, Pauline laughed out loud and Paul hung back, shyly smiling. Both children had large green eyes with long lashes and smooth brown skin. Pauline wore a long skirt, pinned tight at the waist, an over-sized brightly colored blouse and black lace-up shoes a couple of sizes too large. She had shoulder-length, shiny-straight dark hair, darting eyes and an over-bite. I also had an overbite, but Pauline's was a bit more serious, or at least I wanted to think so. Her ears popped out a little from her head and she never stopped smiling or laughing. She talked constantly and her voice was big and loud. She never stopped moving, jumping up from her desk to exclaim or loudly comment on something and often running to one of the classroom windows to catch whatever action might be happening outside.

Paul was slight and much smaller than Pauline. He wore grown-up trousers, clinched tightly at the waist by a belt and rolled up at the ankles, and an adult sweater with the sleeves turned up. On his feet, he wore small tennis shoes that probably pinched with every step he took. Like his sister, Paul didn't wear socks. His hair was shaved close to his head —a style worn by most of the boys in the classroom. He also had an overbite, but his ears were close to his head. While

Pauline was constant motion and words, Paul was quiet and still with a small smile that never left his face. He obviously hero-worshipped his sister, as seen by how he brightened every time Pauline jumped up from her seat and loudly exclaimed over some wondrous discovery she had just made.

Our routine was totally shattered with the constant interruptions from Pauline. Pauline was never mean or unkind, she just couldn't control her enthusiasm, and she was enthusiastic about everything. No amount of admonishments or punishments from Mrs. L. could temper Pauline's outbursts. While Paul quietly worked his assignments, Pauline found something to laugh about, comment on, or a reason to race to the window during every lesson. Mrs. L. was beside herself. Nothing worked—not sitting Pauline in the corner, sending her to the principal's office, denying recess, public humiliation—but nothing stopped Pauline. The rest of the class, me included, hung somewhere between being embarrassed and being entertained by her behavior, which was our main topic of conversation during lunch and breaks. We weren't being unkind, just amazed.

Because Pauline also rode my school bus, my days were all about observing Pauline, to the point that my mother requested I talk about anything other than Pauline at dinner. Pauline and her brother lived on the "across the bridge" school bus route. Right before the First Presbyterian Church, the bus took a right hand turn, drove down a long, straight and often dusty dirt road. Just after it crossed the Swannanoa river bridge, the bus stopped to pick up Paul and Pauline. They lived in a house that was next to the river—one of the ones my father worried about when the river rose. Paul and Pauline were the only children at that bus stop. Pauline always stomped up the steps in her too-large shoes, constantly talking and making comments to the children already on the bus. She always breezed by my seat, smelling like fresh sunshine and kerosene. Paul always followed quietly behind her with his sweet, quiet smile, often tripping over his too-large trousers.

The second "across the river" stop picked up several children from many different families. Pauline kept these children and those of us picked up earlier from Riddle Road constantly laughing at her, but not unkindly, because laughter was what she sought. She loved an audience. Paul was her biggest fan, laughing quietly at her jokes and looking at her with absolute adoration.

One morning, Pauline boarded the bus without her usual noise and clatter. We had been experiencing extremely cold and windy weather for several days. Instead of smelling like sunshine and kerosene, Pauline only smelled like kerosene as she passed by my seat. It was too cold for any of us to smell like sunshine. She usually sat in the middle of the bus, but this morning she went to the back and Paul quietly followed. Even as the other children boarded the bus and sat near her, she remained quiet. A few kids yelled out at her, hoping to stir up some funny banter, but to no avail. I turned to look at her and noticed that she was sitting on her hands. So was Paul.

After the bus dropped us off at the upper elementary building, Pauline and Paul entered the classroom as quietly as they had entered the bus. Mrs. L. was probably thanking her lucky stars and wondering why Pauline was being so well behaved. That morning, as we worked on our social studies workbooks, Mrs. L. walked up and down the aisles, commenting on and correcting our work. When she got to Pauline's desk, she stopped. This wasn't so unusual because Pauline, who was actually good at math, was not good at social studies, mostly because she didn't really care about social studies and therefore always needed help with her workbook. But Mrs. L. didn't say anything this particular morning. Instead, she stared down for a full minute and then with her one hand, gently pulled one of Pauline's hands from under the desk to get a good look at it. Pauline's hands were so severely chapped that they were cracked and bleeding. Pauline started to cry and for a minute, we thought Mrs. L. would cry as well. The room was stone-cold silent. We didn't know that Pauline even knew how to cry nor had we ever seen Mrs. L. show emotion. It was almost too much information to process. With her free hand, Pauline tried to wipe away the tears that were flowing down her face, but it must have stung, because she flung her hand out, wiped it on her adult-sized dress and cried all the harder.

The look on Mrs. L's face was burned into my memory. The sharp features had always been hard as a rock, but now were filled with something I didn't quite understand. Mrs. L. said something softly to Pauline and then walked over to Paul's desk. The same drama was re-enacted yet a second time. Mrs. L. took Paul by the arm, motioned to Pauline and both children left the room with her. As soon as they walked out the door, the buzz of our voices grew louder and louder. We didn't know what to wonder about the most—that Pauline wasn't her laughing, loud, joking self or that Mrs. L. was suddenly on their side. It was like the world was off its orbit.

Our buzz dissolved to whispers and we all anxiously watched the door for their return. After what seemed forever, Paul, Pauline and Mrs. L. returned to the classroom. Mrs. L. entered first with the two children following her through the doorway, their shoulders touching and leaning into each other. They quietly took their seats as Mrs. L. walked to the front of the room. She fully had our attention like never before.

Mrs. L. cleared her throat and started talking about the weather and wind and what it can do to your skin. She said it was especially harmful to go outside on a cold day when your hands are wet, that we should dry them thoroughly and always put on gloves. Almost as one, every student in the class turned to look at Paul and Pauline. You could've heard a pin drop. Then Pauline laughed, which broke the tension in the classroom.

During their time out of the room, Mrs. L. had taken both children to Mrs. Penland's office, the school nurse, where she found Vaseline to rub into their hands. The next day, Mrs. L.

brought Jergen's lotion, Vaseline, gloves, and socks – all new. These items were quietly transferred to Paul and Pauline during a recess break and the rest of the class wouldn't have known about them, except Pauline proudly showed us all of her new items. For her, it was like Christmas.

We all felt differently toward Mrs. L., Paul and Pauline. Friendlier, happier. We no longer watched in quiet amazement as Mrs. L. performed the chalk-eraser exchange trick. Instead, we would raise our hands and say, "do that trick again!" We no longer watched in embarrassment when Pauline jumped up laughing and ran to the window. Instead, we laughed with her. Mrs. L. smiled more and she was actually pretty! And somehow, all of our school work was done and we learned math, spelling, social studies and everything else that sixth graders were required to learn.

We started having "sharing time," a time when Mrs. L. allowed any student to come to the front of the class and share a story, an event or a special item. Pauline always had something to share and she usually had a polite, accepting audience in the rest of us. But her sharing time took a turn for the even better. Pauline was a born entertainer and she coerced Paul in practicing the song, "There's a Hole in the Bucket", to sing in front of the class. As shy as Paul was, he was a natural performer when standing in front of the class next to his sister. Pauline sang Liza's part and Paul sang Henry's.

In the song, Henry sings to Liza that there's a hole in his bucket and Liza responds by telling him to fix it. Henry asks "with what" and Liza answers, "with straw"; Henry asks how shall he cut the straw and Liza tells him with a knife. Henry asks with what shall he sharpen the knife; Liza tells him, with a stone. Henry sings that it's too dry; Liza tells him, then wet it. Henry asks how to get the water and Liza tells him with a bucket, and Henry's response is, "but there is a HOLE in the bucket!"

No matter how often Paul and Pauline sang "There's a Hole in the Bucket", we all laughed uproariously at the circular punch line. Not only did they both dramatize with eye rolls, hands on hips and head tosses, but they could really sing. Their voices weren't just loud and strong; they were on key, in tune and had natural control. We always clapped hard after each performance and both of them always smiled wide, with pure joy written all over their faces.

Paul and Pauline disappeared as fast as they came. After attending our school for a few months, one day they didn't get on the bus and didn't show up at school. It was rumored that there was a fire at their house, that a kerosene heater had tipped over. Everyone got out of the house unharmed, but their family could no longer live in the house. Paul and Pauline were going to live with relatives in another school district. School wasn't as much fun after they left. The sparkle had gone and we were left with math, spelling and social studies and only the chalk-eraser exchange trick for entertainment.

Mrs. Hipps finally returned in the spring and we all gave Mrs. L. tight hugs when she left. Although we were very happy to see our dear and cherished Mrs. Hipps, the loss of Mrs. L. hit us hard. Some of us even cried.

As a group, we realized that we had experienced something so precious and even transforming, that we would hold the memory for a long time. A woman with one hand came into our lives, and we as a class had shown her absolutely no compassion, and yet she had a world of compassion for two children whose own hands were cracked and bleeding because they had no gloves. Not only did Mrs. L. teach us a life lesson, but she might have changed the futures of Paul and Pauline.

Postscript:
I always wondered what happened to Paul and Pauline. I like to think that they are both in the music industry, laughing lots, making tons of money, and never again worried about chapped hands.

PAPER BOY
Keith Gant
1944 and 1945
Buckeye Cove, N.C.
Excerpt from *Don't Tell Mama*
by Keith Gant

A Buckeye Cove paper route was open and my older brother, a paper deliverer, told the route manager that I was twelve years old and needed the job. The fact was, I was only ten years old and when asked by the route manager, I told him my age. I received the job anyway, and was given the names of the customers. The papers I had to carry outweighed me by several pounds.

My father was critically ill and there was little income coming into our family. The route manager was a very kind and pleasant man. To this day, I remain thankful that we met and that he trusted me by giving me a much-needed job, which helped my mother and family.

World War II was underway and the newspaper was the best source of communication about the war. The radio was a good source and was very informative, but the newspaper gave more details. The paper was in great demand and I was now in business. My faithful and feisty dog, Jiggs, was with me as my protector as we carried the news about the Great War.

Buckeye Cove's paper route was about three walking miles long and it took me two hours to deliver my papers. Since the papers had to be on everyone's doorstep before six am, that meant waking up well before four am. Since my father was sick, so it was my mother who woke me every morning. I didn't quite understand it at the time, but he was dying of colon cancer.

Every morning, I left my house and walked to US Highway 70 to pick up my papers, left there for me in a large covered box which was delivered by the Asheville Citizen Times Company truck driver.

With my papers in my bag, Jiggs and I set forth to deliver the latest news to each customer. The road we traveled turned south from the Buckeye Cove bridge, weaving and turning to the left, making a large circle until we returned to our house. Jiggs and I had to ford two creeks while making our route.

Since this was wartime, I was well aware that my customers had family in the military that they wanted to read about and to have knowledge of their safety. One section of the paper listed the names of the missing in action, prisoners of war, and killed in action. The paper was very important and I was doing my part in the war effort.

After several months of working my route, my father's name appeared in the very paper that I was delivering. After a two year illness, Father passed from this life to his Father's House on September 12, 1944. Late that evening, the route manager arrived at my house to pick up the receipts for the papers. I sat in his car trying to decide whether or not to tell him my father had just died. I decided not to and I've always regretted that. Later, after learning of my father's passing, he asked me why I hadn't told him. I had no answer.

After my father's death, I continued delivering the papers. My mother needed the money even more than before. One morning, Jiggs and I arrived at the highway to pick up the papers. As I was putting them in my bag, I looked up to see a large truck coming up the highway and it passed me. As I looked for Jiggs, I saw him run across the road in front of the truck. The driver of the truck didn't slow down, but hit Jiggs. I screamed, "Stop, stop! You killed my dog!" I rushed to Jiggs after dropping my papers to the ground, knelt down and picked up his lifeless body, crying and pleading for him not to die. I carried Jiggs across the bridge, went up the bank and placed his still body on a carpet of tall, dried grass. I promised Jiggs I would be back to bury him when I completed my route. I continued my route, crying, hurt because I'd lost my best friend and the driver didn't even stop. Having just lost my father, the loss of my dog was overwhelming.

I completed my route and returned to our house without Jiggs. I told my mother that a truck hit him and I had to go back and bury him. My mother looked surprised and then told me wonderful news, "Jiggs isn't dead! Jiggs is underneath the house. He's hurt, but not dead."

I crawled under the house, took Jiggs in my arms and thanked him for being alive, knowing that God had answered my prayers. I couldn't give Jiggs up so soon after losing my father. We didn't have money to take Jiggs to a veterinarian, but he recovered soon and was by my side as I delivered papers; I loved him more than ever. I had prayed that he would live, would get well, and God answered my prayers, showing He cared about little boys and their dogs.

Not only did my dog live, but good fortune came. Meeting the paper route manager of Moore General Hospital opened the door to a greater opportunity. I had an offer to sell papers at the hospital. I started out with the evening edition of the Asheville Citizen Times, which arrived in time for me to work after school and return home in the evening. Soon a morning route at the hospital opened and I convinced the route manager that I could sell papers in the morning before school.

Going to school and selling papers in the hospital proved to be challenging and difficult, but the extra hardship made me determined to work hard and help my mother. One of the advantages of selling papers at Moore General was that I was working inside, out of the severe winter weather. The disadvantage was what I saw inside the hospital. I knew wounded soldiers were in the hospital for treatment, and although I had watched my father die a slow and painful death, I wasn't prepared to witness how war destroyed the human body and spirit. The bravery of these men made me want to grow up and be a soldier and fight for our freedom.

Pressed in my memory is the kindness of a nurse who extended to me great compassion. Every morning, I left my house very early, without breakfast and often hungry. I arrived at the nurses' dining hall and left the newspapers on the table with a dish. The staff came in, bought a paper and placed the correct change in the dish. And also every morning, a beautiful nurse came into the hall and told me to go to the pantry and she would bring me breakfast. She hid me in the pantry so other staff would not know that I was eating. She was breaking the rules by feeding me. The pantry had a good smell. On the shelves were spices, coffee, sugar and things that my family could not buy because of the war. Even without the war, my father had been the breadwinner, and since he had passed, we had no steady income. All of the Moore General Hospital staff treated me with kindness and respect and I will forever be grateful. But that nurse will remain in my memory forever—she was God's angel who came to help me.

One day, I had just returned home when the route manager drove up in our yard and said, 'Get in. We have an extra to sell."

"JAPS QUIT" read the headlines. "Japs quit, Japs quit!" I hollered as I entered the hospital, selling my papers to a celebrating, rejoicing, war-weary group of wounded soldiers. That night, they were crying and singing. They were so relieved that the war with Japan was finally over.

Postscript:

Keith Gant, my uncle, passed away on June 29, 2013. This story is taken from "Don't Tell Mama, Memories of a Mountain Boy Growing up too Fast", written and self-published by Keith in 2004. After serving in the U.S. Air Force, Keith entered the ministry in the late 1950s. He married a terrific woman, raised two wonderful sons and enjoyed being involved in the lives of two beautiful grandchildren.

He treasured his framed front page of the Asheville Citizen Times special edition with the news of Japan's surrender.

—Nancy Fowler

HAIR REVOLT
Nadine Wells
1967
Lansing, Michigan

When I was about 16 years old, my morning routine usually went something like this: wake up, eat breakfast, brush teeth, apply eyeliner, mascara, blush, lip gloss. Use ratting comb to tease hair up high, put on school uniform. Walk to school, enter doors, be greeted by Sister Margaret Mary, who then immediately took me to the girls' room to scrub my face free of all makeup, remove my comb from my purse and roughly yank at my hair until it was tangle free and flat. Girls entering the bathroom were always horrified and quickly retreated to avoid the same treatment. I can still smell and feel the brown paper towels and harsh hand soap she used to scrub my face. I'm not sure why I tried to sneak by Sister every morning, but I always held out hope that she wouldn't catch me.

Next came Home Room with roll call attendance and dress inspection. Students suspected of rolling up their uniform skirt above the knees were required to kneel in front of the all-girl class. If a skirt did not reach the floor or a sweater was too tight, these hussies were sent to the office. I quickly learned how to make my uniform match my shiny, make up free face and flat hairdo (stretch the skirt waist out, pull down on hips, roll up and safety pin after the inspection period).

Along with all my girl friends, I was very interested in makeup and hairdos. When we visited each other, away from Monsignor Gabriels High School, we swapped makeup and gave each other new hair dos that we saw movie stars wearing. We weren't shallow, silly girls. Actually, we were good students. We just liked feeling glamorous—all the more so because we weren't allowed any glamour at school. I had no problems with the way I looked. In fact, my dad liked calling me his "little Indian girl." I don't know if we had any Native American ancestry; all I ever knew about were my Swedish grandparents, but out of a family of fair-haired girls, I was the one girl with very dark hair and the ability to tan well. My brothers were a mix of fair and dark, but my sisters were all very fair. I was perfectly happy with my looks, but I was 16—the age of trying new things. My need to try a new look ended up causing me a lot of trouble and not a little embarrassment.

We were all impressed when an older school friend enrolled in cosmetology school. Marsha was actually going to school to learn how to do makeup and hair. Sounded a lot better than math and science. She wanted to practice her skills and she had no problem finding volunteers. Of course, at that point, she didn't have a lot of experience, but my friends and I were more than happy to let her practice what she had learned on us.

I was really excited when Marsha invited me over to her house one day after school. She was going to give me a new hair color. I imagined myself as a gorgeous platinum blond, with long bouncing curls that I would carelessly fling across my shoulder. This would be something that Sister Margaret Mary could not make me wash off!

I sat down in Marsha's kitchen chair and watched her mix a concoction of something that smelled vile. She painted my hair with it and then covered my head with a plastic shower cap. I sat for what seemed hours until she finally pulled the cap off and shampooed my hair in her kitchen sink. She combed my hair out, rolled it in curlers, put the hair dryer bonnet on my head and turned it on. I just couldn't wait to see the new me!

After some time, she took off the dryer bonnet, unrolled the curlers and brushed out my hair. Not until then did she let me look at myself in the mirror. My hair was more than platinum; it was pretty much white. I blinked my eyes, tilted my head to the right and then the left, but the color didn't change. It was still pretty much white.

I thanked her and told her I had to run to be home in time for dinner. I started thinking about how my parents might react to my new hair color, especially since I hadn't told them what I was going to do. I had figured I would cross that bridge when I got to it, but that bridge was fast approaching.

It was just starting to get dark when I arrived at our front door and the door was already locked. I knew Mom wasn't home from work yet and Dad was cooking dinner, which smelled pretty good from where I was standing. I knocked on the door and watched Dad come to open it. He pulled the door open and his jaw quite literally dropped. He was speechless. So was I. I wanted him to say something first, which he finally did. "Who are you? I have no daughters with white hair!" He then slammed the door shut and locked it again.

So there I stood. I didn't know if he was kidding or really angry, I just knew I was hungry, had homework and wanted to go inside. Just as I was trying to figure out my next steps, my mother pulled up in the driveway. I knew this wasn't going to be good.

After asking me in a variety of loud ways what in the world was I thinking, she brought me inside and told me that

I absolutely was not going to school the next day. Instead, I was going down to the drugstore to get a box of brown dye to try and get back to my natural hair color. By that time, my scalp was developing small blisters and I wasn't relishing the idea of putting more chemicals on it, but decided compliance was the easiest path.

The next morning, I was at the drug store as soon as it opened. I bought a box of dark brown hair color that, from the picture at least, looked like my real hair. When I got home, everyone else was either at work or school so I had the house to myself, which allowed me to change back to brown in quiet misery.

The results were less than spectacular. My hair had turned kind of an Army green, or "puke green" as one of my brothers called it when he got home. I wasn't sure what to do next, all I knew was that instead of feeling like a glamorous beauty, I felt like someone with green hair and a burning scalp.

My mother had little sympathy when she got home. She called my older brother's girlfriend, Claudia, who was also attending beauty school. Claudia came over and brought her professional hair colors and warned me of possible scalp pain. By the time she was finished, my hair looked better, but my scalp was burning up. I didn't dare say anything, figuring my parents were unhappy enough with me. But I knew I would not be teasing my hair anytime soon as the thought of Sister Mary Margaret combing the ratted hair brought tears to my eyes.

My scalp eventually healed, but not without many days of pain. My biggest disappointment was that I didn't get to go to school and watch Sister's face as she realized she could not wash out my hair color. I suppose she could have sent a note home to my parents, but that couldn't have made things much worse than they already were.

I would like to say that there was a life lesson from this experience, but I think the only lesson I took away from it was that if you chemically treat your hair three times in two days, you're going to feel pain. Oh yeah, and I no longer want to have white hair.

Postscript:

As a grown-up, Nadine never varied much from her original color. Although envious of her friend's beauty school education, Nadine completed an undergraduate degree in Advertising and Public Relations and a graduate degree in Management. After retiring from a career working for the Department of Defense, Nadine enjoys volunteering with non-profit organizations, traveling with her husband, and time with their extended family.

FOOD AND FUN
Talmadge Burnette
1932
Bee Tree, N.C.
Excerpt from *Looking Back*
by Talmadge Burnette

An important item in the diet of the mountain people of Western North Carolina during the depression was molasses, and Daddy was a master molasses maker. Molasses were made in the fall before frost came. We planted our molasses cane in rows, like corn and it was cultivated the same way. In the fall, the leaves (fodder) were stripped off and tied into bundles. It was dried and fed to the milk cows, for it was an excellent milk maker. If it frosted on the cane, it was no good for the making of molasses.

You had to be careful when pulling the fodder because there was a worm that fed on it called a "pack saddle" and he had little stickers all over him that would sting you. His sting was very painful. He was the same color as the fodder and was hard to see. After the fodder was pulled, the cane stalks were cut down, and the seed heads cut off. The seed heads were also cow feed as well as chicken feed.

The molasses making place was on Horace Morgan's farm about two miles from our house. We hauled the cane to the making place on a mule and a sled. It would take several trips to get all of the cane there. There was a mill that consisted of a steel roller that turned against another steel roller powered by a mule that walked around and around, turning the rollers.

My job was to put the cane stalks into the mill where the juice was squeezed out and ran into a barrel. There was a furnance nearby with a large rectangular metal pan on it. The furnace was fired with wood, and the juice was boiled down to molasses in this pan. The juice was dipped out of the barrel with a bucket and poured into the pan. It took quite a while for the juice to boil down to molasses and the top of the juice had to be skimmed continuously. This was done with a square piece of metal that looked like a shovel with a wooden handle. The skimmings were green colored and couldn't be left on the molasses. The skimmer was pushed along the top of the juice, catching the skimmings and then emptied into a bucket.

The molasses season would last for about two weeks and was a community affair. Every one who had molasses to make and a lot who didn't would be there. Country folks had a way of making work into a social gathering, and the molasses making lasted far into the night. Molasses had to be cooked just the right length of time. If cooked too long, they were black and too thick. If not cooked long enough, there were green and too thin. Daddy could tell just how long to cook them, and he and Uncle Murray Howie did just about all of the cooking.

Horace Morgan had several "sheep nose" apple trees and the apples were always ripe at molasses time. There were delicious and kids would always raid the trees. The kids would also break off a joint of cane, put I cross ways in their mouth, and twist each end. This would force the sweet juice into their mouths. Another fun thing was to take a stalk of cane, put it in the furnace until it got hot, then strike it real hard on the ground. I would explode with a sound like a gunshot.

After the molasses were made they had to be put into containers. In those days, shortening came in tin buckets with a tight fitting lid and a wire bail or handle. They came in two sizes, gallon and half-gallon. All of these buckets were saved and used as water buckets, milk buckets, berry picking buckets, and molasses buckets. We would make thirty or forty gallons of molasses. Some we sold for fifty cents a gallon to those who didn't make their own, and the rest we stored for our own use. As well as the buckets, some were stored in glass gallon jugs. The last year that we made molasses was 1935. Daddy was working regularly at Beacon and didn't have time to devote to all of the work that it took to make them.

Another chore that was turned into fun was corn shucking. Farmers would gather their corn in the filed, load it on a sled or wagon, haul it near the corn crib, and pile it in a big pile. A crib was a storage building, made from three or four-inch boards, placed about an inch apart when put up. This allowed air to circulate and dry the corn. They would invite the neighbors of the community in some night for a "corn shucking." Kerosene lanterns would be hung around in various places for light, because no one had electricity. Everyone would jump in and start shucking corn and throwing it in the crib.

If you found a red ear, you got to kiss the girl of your choice. The corn was white, but usually there would be red ears popping up. Some folks accused some of the young fellows of bringing red ears with them.

After the corn was shucked, there was usually a square dance. Musicians in the community were always invited and told to bring their instruments. I have heard of some putting a jug of corn liquor in the bottom of the pile of corn. This was supposed to make the shuckers work faster, each one trying to get to the bottom of the pile and the jug. I was never at a corn shucking where this occurred. There was no such thing as television and very few radios in the community. Country people had their own old-fashioned, clean entertainment.

Postscript:
Talmadge Burnette was my father. He passed away March 1, 2003 at 84 years. The above description is from his book, "Looking Back," which was published in 1997 and then again in 2001. He entered the Army in 1941, achieved the rank of captain in 1943 and was medically discharged in 1945 after contracting TB. He became a business owner and real estate developer. With our mom, he raised my brothers and me to enjoy many of his same childhood adventures. We were mighty lucky to have had him and our mom as parents.

—Nancy Fowler

TOOTSIE IN CHARGE
Sandy Montgomery
1958
Broken Arrow, Oklahoma

Teenage girls eagerly anticipate and dream about what their prom dress will look like. In the late 50s long, frilly formals with hoop skirts were the rage among the seniors in my high school. My mom and I began talking about what kind of formal I would wear to the senior prom long before I was old enough to attend.

Mom, known as Tootsie to friends and neighbors, was an expert seamstress, one of her many talents. In fact, Mom was a "force of Nature." She was one of those women who could walk into a project, know exactly what needed to be done, make sure everyone completed their role and not walk away until everything was complete. If Mom had been in the Army, she would've been the General. She always made Easter dresses and school clothes for my sister, Jan, and me. She spent hours and hours sewing tiny ruffles on our prom dresses.

The year that I was a senior in high school Mom was confined to a hospital bed due to tuberculosis. I learned to cook that year. Previous to her illness, I was busy with going to speech contests, playing in the band and serving as editor of Tiger Tales. I was always asked to set the table and make the tea, but those skills did not serve my family very well while Mom was confined to bed and there were hungry mouths to be fed.

My dad loved corn bread. He didn't get to enjoy his favorite bread for almost two years because I was a miserable failure at making corn bread. There were no Jiffy mixes at that time.

During Mom's sickness, our family left the farm and moved to town. She hadn't seen the new house, but the first thing she had moved into the new house was her hospital bed. Yes, even when she was flat of her back, she was still very much in charge.

Her bed was located in the living room where she could see the stove, which had push buttons that showed the different colors according to the temperature. She gave orders from her hospital bed as I attempted to learn to cook during my senior year in high school.

When the time of the senior prom drew near, I began to be concerned about what I was going to wear. I should never have worried because Mom was still very much in charge. One evening she asked Dad to move the sewing machine to the living room beside her bed. I wondered what in the world she was going to do. Did this have something to do with my prom dress?

Mom sent me to the store to pick out a pattern for the formal and buy the material. I had no idea that I was selecting one of the most difficult patterns. I simply knew that the pattern I had selected was very much in style.

When we returned home Mom started giving Dad directions for cutting out the pattern. That was quite an ordeal but Dad, who was always a man of few words, knew how to follow Mom's directions. We learned after Dad's death why he was such a quiet man ... our mom always had a lot to say which left little time for him to speak except to say, "whatever you want to do Tootsie, is fine with me." The thing that best describes our dad is that he was an "iron hand inside a velvet glove". He always let Mom think she was in charge but ultimately he was in charge and a very wise man at that.

Mom gave Dad instructions each evening about how to sew the formal. After a long day at work as a planner at American Airlines, he returned home to become a seamstress. Mom gave specific directions for him to stitch the black formal which had tiny ruffles all the way down the full skirt that was held out by hoops and a number of "can cans" that had been made during my junior year by Nana, as my mom would later be called.

The most precious gift of all was given to me—a persistent mom who was not about to let me not be the "belle of the ball" and a dad who knew how to follow directions so that his little girl would have the loveliest of all prom dresses. That dress was a perfect example of unselfish, unconditional love.

Postscript:
The greatest joy of Sandy's life has always been to make a difference in the lives of children. She spent ten years as a fifth grade teacher and twenty nine years as an administrator in Tulsa and Broken Arrow Public Schools. After retirement she became a textbook consultant. She later served as adjunct professor and mentor to teachers completing their internship at Northeastern State University. Sandy is an avid reader, knitter and a "fair-weather" gardener. She never learned to sew but does have an old-fashioned treadle sewing machine and a newer Singer machine just in case she decides to learn to sew in her spare time.

THE FIGHTING FIELD
Richard Burnette
1956
Swannanoa, N.C.

For several years, our family grew and sold strawberries so we could buy a family season pass at Asheville's Recreation Park swimming pool. The deal our parents cut with us kids was that we would work in the strawberry patch—weeding, hoeing, picking berries—and the money earned from selling the strawberries would go towards paying for the season pass. We thought this to be a great idea; we loved spending hot summer days at the big Rec Park pool with friends and we also had some pride in the fact that our strawberry money paid for it. In addition, the strawberry field was a pleasant place to work. But on one hot summer on a Wednesday, our strawberry field became a fighting field, a place for an angry showdown among friends over a misunderstanding that I fear I caused.

The year was 1956 and in our small community, businesses closed on Wednesday afternoons. This was a carry-over from WWII, when businesses closed one afternoon a week so that the employees could tend to their victory gardens. Swannanoa continued the practice long after its need had ended. This meant that our dad got home early on Wednesdays and we usually either helped Dad with work around our ten acres or we did something fun. On this particular Wednesday, Dad promised to take me, my older brother, Butch, and Harry Gibbs, fishing at Curtis Creek. Harry was helping us pull weeds between the rows of strawberries while we waited on Dad.

Harry, Tom and David Gibbs had been friends of ours for many years. We had all been in Scouts together since we were Cubs and our parents also socialized together. The two families had taken many camping trips together and we'd always enjoyed their company and friendship. The five of us made a rowdy bunch of boys, often laughing, pushing, shoving and just generally engaging in good-natured horse play.

On this Wednesday, with a hot sun beating down on me and what seemed to be endless weeds in front of me, I was sure the work was never going to end and that it would be hours before Dad got home. I straightened up and looked at Butch and Harry, both all bent over and quietly focused on their work. I kicked at a large dirt clod and looked again at Butch. His back was to me as he bent toward the ground, grabbing big handfuls of weeds. The target his backside presented was just too tempting and I figured we needed some action to break the monotony of work.

I picked up the dirt clod and took good aim at Butch's behind. Just before the clod made impact, Butch started to stand up. My aim wasn't as good as I thought it was and I also threw clod harder than I'd meant to. Added to that, Butch didn't have his feet well anchored as he straightened out. All of these factors converged so that when the dirt clod hit him, it struck his lower back instead of his behind, threw him off balance and pushed him face down into a row of old strawberry plants and dirt. Harry quickly stood up and watched as Butch pulled himself off the ground.

When Butch turned and looked me in the eye, I immediately knew he didn't see that dirt clod as a fun diversion to break the monotony of work. His eyes were narrowed, his chin extended, fists clenched and he was taking a step towards me. Butch was two and half years older than me and probably about 10 pounds heavier. I knew I didn't have a chance, so without even thinking, I pulled off the best protective defense possible—without saying a word, I pointed at Harry. Butch didn't so much as pause, but jumped on Harry with his arms and fists flying. Harry was a better match for Butch than I was, and the punches on both sides were becoming intense.

Mom had stepped out of the house to see how we were all doing and saw the whole episode. She stopped the fight before the blood started flowing, but not before feelings were profoundly hurt. Harry had ridden his bicycle to our house and he jumped on it and furiously peddled home. Butch and I walked up to the house with Mom. About the same time, Dad pulled into the driveway. He'd passed Harry on the road and knew something wasn't quite right. We sat down while Mom and Dad got to the bottom of the story which meant I was in big trouble. Although it was evident that I was the instigator of the fight, they made it clear that Butch also owed an apology because he landed the first blow. I guess I had shame, but I wasn't trying to start a fight—I just wanted to start a fun tussle to break the monotony of pulling weeds. It just didn't turn out as I had anticipated.

Dad put Butch and me in the car and we went to Harry's house and apologized to him. Facing Harry was a tense moment. He listened politely, but anger was still written all over his face. I didn't think he believed that I threw that clod. Our friendship after that time was awkward and Butch and Harry never quite seemed to be as close of friends as they were before. It was a tough lesson learned.

Believe it or not, we did go fishing with Harry that Wednesday. We also listened to lectures from both Mom and Dad about how we had risked an important friendship—not just our personal friendships, but a bigger friendship between two families. I also do remember that I had intense solo weeding duty for several weeks.

Postscript:
More than 50 years have passed since that fight in the strawberry field. The Burnette kids have great memories of the Gibbs boys and their adventures. And Harry, if you are reading this, Richard really did throw that clod and Butch is innocent. And also, they are both really sorry.

ABOUT THIS BOOK

It is goal of this book to promote the need for childhood cancer research and the excellent mission of the Scott Carter Foundation. The project provided additional, and unexpected, benefits to me personally—I learned more about my family and friends, made new friends and totally enjoyed reading (and in some cases, listening to) every story.

It is hoped that the experiences in this book provide an entertaining read, especially for our children and grandchildren. It is also hoped that our grandchildren, great-grandchildren, and all the generations beyond, enjoy their childhood adventures in good health.

—Nancy Burnette Fowler
August 2013
Naples, Florida